Family Recipes

Saving the world one recipe at a time

Martie Kraus, Valayne May, Kerri Hamblin, Jana Chapman

iUniverse, Inc.
Bloomington

Family Recipes
Saving the world one recipe at a time

iUniverse books may be ordered through booksellers or by contacting:

iUniverse
1663 Liberty Drive
Bloomington, IN 47403
www.iuniverse.com
1-800-Authors (1-800-288-4677)

ISBN: 978-1-4502-7918-5 (sc)
ISBN: 978-1-4502-7919-2 (ebk)

Printed in the United States of America

iUniverse rev. date: 4/26/2011

This is not your average cookbook. Although we don't want to discourage anyone from using this book and enjoying the great recipes contained in it, it may be more useful to those who have some cooking experience. We have not given detailed instructions for preparation for most recipes. For that reason, some basic knowledge of food preparation and experience in the kitchen is helpful. We want people to use this book to add to their own favorite recipes and make these recipes their own by modifying and adjusting them to meet their own tastes and preferences. We love to do that to recipes we find and try.

The recipes in this book have been begged, borrowed, modified, and shared from many sources. We are the kind of cooks who gather recipes from friends, family, and other sources; try them at home on your own families, then pass them along to others. We have tried to give credit to friends and family who have helped make us the cooks we are, but we have some recipes that have been in our family for years and have no idea as to their origin. We also usually change recipes we get and therefore they become something different and unique. We invite you to do the same. Use these recipes; change them; make them your own; share them with others.

Our families tend to be on the picky side and many of our recipes do not include onions. We don't really like them. (It is a texture thing more than a taste thing.) This is a great example of how you can take these great ideas for food and make them your own. We use a lot of onion powder, but very few real onions – it's a family thing. Our grandma used to try to trick us by grating onions into her meatloaf and other dishes. Sometimes it worked and sometimes it didn't. Our mother tried similar things with powdered milk and deer meat – neither one of those worked. There is no hiding the taste or texture of venison or reconstituted powdered milk when you have such picky eaters! We have made and eaten every recipe in this book on more than one occasion. Some recipes have been in our family for generations. We feel confident you can open this book and make any recipe and come out with a great product. We have personally tested every one (well, I can't say we have all eaten the sweet and sour tuna, but my sister Kerri has and she lived through it. That is the only recipe we would not recommend even though we have included it!)

We have had books, recipe cards, pieces of paper, and newspaper clippings of recipes for years, and we finally decided it would be great to have many of our favorite recipes in one easy to use place for a change. We really made this book for us, but we hope whoever happens to use it enjoys the first offering from our collection. We are always on the look out for new recipes to try and invite anyone who would like to send us their favorite recipes to do so at the email address below. We hope this is just the first of many cookbooks that hold our favorite recipes. Maybe yours will be in our next one. Send your favorite recipes to sistersfamilyrecipes@gmail.com.

We certainly enjoy a good meal out now and then, but we believe the best meals are those made with love and eaten with people you enjoy spending time with. When you cook, you get to decide what goes into everything you make. You see how fresh *things are. You get to smell all the great fragrances of cooking food. You get to lick the beater, (we used to fight over that at our house!) and sneak a handful of cookie dough! Think about the last time you had people over. Where does everyone hang out? Usually the kitchen! That is because everyone knows great things come from the kitchen. Cooking makes you feel creative. Cooking with someone else brings you closer together. There are so many great memories connected to the food we eat and their smells. So many family traditions are connected to certain foods at specific times. It is never too late to start a family tradition connected to food or add a new kind of food to a traditional holiday or event.*

We think we really can change the world one freshly baked cookie at a time. We have seen first hand the difference one cookie can make in the life of a child or an adult. Giving makes you feel good; giving something you made yourself makes you feel great! Giving is a good feeling and giving of one's self is a great thing to do. Make a batch of cookies, maybe even a double batch, mix up some bread, find someone to give to, and change the part of the world you live in.

Desserts

We started with dessert because dessert is a signature of our family. How many times have you wished you **had** saved room for dessert? We always do, and sometimes we even start with it. I wouldn't be lying to say that many a vacation has been planned around where we would eat dessert. When our family gets together, there is always something great to eat. This has been the case for generations. When we were very young, our family was known for bringing homemade desserts to every family get-together.

Our mom is famous for her pies and ice cream. There wasn't a McGee family holiday get-together without one or the other and sometimes both. We always do things in a big way and we never make "a" pie. Our favorite piecrust recipe makes three crusts, so the minimum is always three. At Thanksgiving we always had to make a fruit pie for Uncle George. None of us really like fruit (well, except for Jana), but cooking and baking are not usually about what you like but about making things that other people will enjoy. We still start making pies several days before Thanksgiving. We start by making piecrusts and freezing them. Then, the night before Thanksgiving, we fill the crusts and bake the pies.

Sunday nights are the perfect time to make something sweet to eat. We usually have a big family meal on Sunday afternoons and then we don't make another meal in the evening. We often have extended family and/or friends over, so dessert is the perfect thing to have around to go with the leftovers from Sunday dinner. Sunday night would not be complete without dessert, and the dessert is always sweeter when it is shared. Sunday night dessert is the perfect way to get ready for the long work week ahead. It really spices up the dulldrums of knowing you have to go back to work in the morning. Mary Poppins was right. A teaspoon of sugar does help the medicine go down!

Desserts also make great gifts. We always make something fun to give to neighbors and friends to mark special occasions and holidays. Christmas is one time of year we make lots of treats to give to those we love and don't often find time to spend with during the year. Our neighbors often did the same. We often participated in neighborhood cookie exchanges (and still do), so our house was full of homemade treats for weeks after Christmas. Our little sister Jana loaded up all the treats we

1

received from friends and neighbors for Christmas one year and sold them back to our neighbors all along our street. She made enough money to buy some chickens and turkeys at a local feed store. We didn't realize what she had done until we heard the crowing from our playhouse in the backyard several weeks later. Our mother was horrified to find out what she had done.

We hope you will enjoy sharing these great desserts with people you care about. They have been shared with people we love at weddings, holidays, for gifts, and just for Sunday evening gatherings. We suggest you bake something once a week. Double the recipe and give some of what you make away. You will have two treats that way!

~ *Pies and Cakes* ~

Super Great Pie Crust
This is a no-fail piecrust recipe. It makes enough for 3 pie shells

3 C flour   1 t salt
1 ½ C shortening   ½ C water
1 egg   1 t vinegar

Blend flour, salt, and shortening with a pastry blender until fine as cornmeal. Beat together water, egg, and vinegar; add to flour mixture. Roll out on floured surface.

Super Great Pie Crust II
This slight variation makes a really flaky pastry. Be careful about measuring the cream of tartar. Adding too much will make the dough difficult to roll out.

3 C flour
⅛ t cream of tartar
1 ½ C shortening   1 t salt
1 egg   ½ C water
        1 t vinegar

Blend flour, salt, and shortening with a pastry blender until fine as cornmeal. Beat together water, egg, and vinegar; add to flour mixture. Roll out on floured surface.

Sistersfamilyrecipes@gmail.com

Pie Crust (for tarts)
This recipe makes enough dough for one tart crust. It is a little sweeter than our Super Great pie crust recipe.

1 C flour	⅓ C butter
dash salt and sugar	1 T lemon juice
1 – 2 T water	1 egg yolk

Blend butter, flour, sugar, and salt with a pastry blender until fine as cornmeal. Beat lemon juice, egg yolk, and water together; add to flour mixture. Shape into round disc and chill for ½ hour or more. Roll out on floured surface.

No Roll Pie Crust
This is an easy recipe that requires no rolling out and transferring to a pie pan, so if you have trouble with that step this is the recipe for you.

1 ½ C flour	1 C shortening
½ C water	½ t salt

Blend shortening into flour and salt. Add water. Pat mixture evenly into bottom and sides of pie pan.

Phyllis's Pie Crust
¾ C shortening	1 t salt
¼ C boiling water	1 T milk
2 C flour	

Whip shortening and water until mixture looks like whipped cream. Add other ingredients and mix to form dough. Divide dough in half and roll out between waxed paper sheets to form crust for bottom and top of pie.

Phyllis's Rosy Apple Pie
6 apples, peeled and cored	1 C flour
1 sm pkg raspberry gelatin	½ C margarine
1 C sugar	

Slice apples in unbaked pie shell. Sprinkle gelatin over apples. Combine sugar, flour, and butter to resemble crumbs and sprinkle over top of pie. Bake at 350 for 45 – 60 minutes.

❧⸱❧

Our mother was known for her pies in our family. They were a staple at Christmas and Thanksgiving. We started making the pie crusts days before the event. After days of work making up to 15 pies for Thanksgiving, we would load the trunk and back window of the family car and make the hour long trek to grandma's house. My dad was always the driver and he liked to drive fast. The trip to grandma's house was much more akin to "Mr. Toad's Wild Ride" than it was to "Over the River and Through the Woods." Our mom would yell at our dad the whole way about starting and stopping too quickly and ruining the pies. We always made it with pies in tact and usually only one or two of the beautiful crusts would be smashed. It was always an eventful experience, and we were glad to get to grandma's house and unload. We would eat a wonderful dinner with our cousins, aunts, and uncles. The boys and men would retire to the backyard to shoot the basketball and the women and girls would do the dishes and make sure everything was put back in grandma's neat and orderly kitchen. We could not eat dessert until all the dishes were done and leftovers put away. Then, my mom would "take orders" for kinds of pie and ice cream and we would be the servers.

<u>Pumpkin Pie</u>

¾ cup granulated sugar
½ t salt
¼ t ground cloves
1 can (15 oz.) Pumpkin
Whipped cream (optional)

1 t ground cinnamon
½ t ground ginger
2 large eggs
1 can (12 fl. oz.) Evaporated Milk
1 unbaked 9-inch (4-cup volume) deep-dish pie shell

Mix sugar, cinnamon, salt, ginger and cloves in small bowl. Beat eggs in large bowl. Stir in pumpkin and sugar-spice mixture. Gradually stir in evaporated milk. Pour into pie shell. Bake in preheated 425° F oven for 15 minutes. Reduce temperature to 350° F; bake for 40 to 50 minutes or until knife inserted near center comes out clean. Cool on wire rack for 2 hours. Serve immediately or refrigerate. Top with sweetened whipped cream before serving.

Pumpkin Chiffon Pie

Mix together in medium saucepan:

1 envelope unflavored gelatin	½ C sugar
½ t salt	½ t cinnamon
½ t allspice	¼ t ginger
¼ t nutmeg	

Stir in:

¾ C. milk	2 slightly beaten egg yolks* (save whites)
1 C. canned pumpkin (not pumpkin pie mix)	

Cook and stir over medium heat until gelatin dissolves and is heated through. Remove from heat and chill until partially set.

While filling is chilling:

Beat the two reserved egg whites* until soft peaks form. Gradually stir in ¼ C. sugar and beat until stiff peak stage.

Whip ½ C whipping cream to stiff peak stage.

When pumpkin filling is cooled, fold whipped egg whites and cream into mixture.

Pour filling into 9-inch graham cracker crust and chill until set.

Walnut Pumpkin Pie

1 – 9 inch graham cracker crust	½ t each ginger, nutmeg, and salt
1 – 15 oz. can of pumpkin	1 – 14 oz. can sweetened condensed milk
¼ C packed brown sugar	1 egg
2 T flour	1 ½ t ground cinnamon (divided into 2-¾s)
2 T margarine	¾ C chopped walnuts

Heat oven to 425 degrees. In large mixing bowl, combine pumpkin, sweetened condensed milk, egg, spices, ¾ t. cinnamon, and salt; mix well. Pour mixture into pie crust and bake for 15 minutes, remove from oven. Reduce oven to 350 degrees. In bowl, combine sugar, flour and remaining cinnamon with softened margarine until crumbly. Stir in walnuts and sprinkle over pie. Return to oven and bake for 40 minutes more or until set.

Thanksgiving would not be complete without this great pie. We had our own pecan trees growing up and we used to pick and shell our own pecans for pie and other desserts. My dad would sit at our kitchen table and shell the nuts while we baked pies in the kitchen. He was always looking for a sheller that would make his job easier and leave the pecan halves in tact. He often ate as many as he shelled! If a recipe calls for nuts, we almost always use pecans – just because we always had them on hand. Walnuts, black walnuts, or almonds are often equally good. We suggest toasting the nuts before using them in most recipes to bring out their natural oils and enhance their flavor.

Pecan Pie

Pastry for 9" pie

3 eggs   ½ t salt
⅔ C sugar   ⅓ C butter, melted
1 C light corn syrup   1 C pecan halves

Heat oven to 375 degrees. Beat eggs, sugar, salt, butter and corn syrup together for 2 minutes. Stir in pecan halves. Pour into pastry-lines pie pan. Bake 40-50 minutes or until set.

(Valayne likes to serve caramel sauce over pumpkin pie and pumpkin tarts. Why not make a good thing even better?)

Blueberry Pie

1 baked 9" pastry shell   ¼ C water
4 C blueberries   1 T margarine
1 C sugar   1 t vanilla
3 T cornstarch

Pour 3 cups of blueberries into pie shell, spread evenly and set aside. Combine remaining berries, sugar, cornstarch, and water in saucepan, cook and stir over low heat until thickened. Remove from heat; stir in margarine and vanilla; cool. Pour over berries in pie shell; chill. Serve with whipped cream or ice cream on top. This recipe is a variation from Butler's Orchard where we picked our own blueberries. They are so sweet and great when you pick them yourself.

Apple Pie 2 Ways

This recipe makes pie filling for 3 pies, or 7-quart jars to can and preserve. It is the best apple pie filling we have tasted. Valayne received a jar of it as a Christmas gift from a friend one year and it has become a family favorite for pie filling and crisps or crumbles. Food always makes a great gift. You'll need about 8 peeled, cored, and sliced apples for this recipe – give or take. It takes 2-3 apples per pie. Granny Smiths are the traditional apples for pies, but we find they have very little flavor. Use the apples you like to eat. Galas and Macintosh are nice. If it tastes great to eat, it will taste great in a pie.

9 C water   3 ½ C sugar

Bring to boil and then add:

1 C sugar   ¼ t nutmeg
¼ t cloves   1 t almond extract
½ t salt

Mix together over medium heat in a large saucepan. Mix 1 C cold water, 3 T lemon juice, and 1 C cornstarch together, then add to mixture in saucepan. Heat mixture until thick and bubbly. Pour over apple slices that are peeled and fill up 7 quart jars. Process jars in hot water bath for 30 minutes. If making pie filling to use immediately, add peeled and sliced apples to saucepan and cook for 5 minutes, then pour into uncooked pie shells. Cover with second crust or streusel topping. Bake at 350 for about an hour. Be sure to place pies on cookie sheet to prevent a messy oven, lots of smoke, and possible fire. I am speaking from experience! It looks great to cut out shapes from top crust and sprinkle with a little cinnamon and sugar.

Streusel Topping

This is the best recipe for crumb topping EVER! We use it whenever we want a crumb topping on anything from muffins to pies to crisps.

¼ C sugar   ⅓ C light brown sugar packed
¼ pound (1 stick) melted unsalted 1 ⅓ C flour
    butter

Mix sugars and flour then pour melted butter in; mix well and place on top of whatever you are making. *For a softer crumb topping, use equal parts butter and flour.

❧ ❧

Doing something with someone else often results in learning something new. We always learn something new when we cook together – either a new recipe or just an added spice or new way of doing something. Valayne's mother-in-law is a wonderful cook. She is from Germany and makes some great authentic dishes. She was recently visiting at Valayne's house and helping to make one of her signature desserts – Poppy Seed Cake. Valayne always had trouble with the crumb topping falling off and getting done before the rest of the cake. Christa told her to moisten the top of the cake with water and *adjust her crumb recipe to have equal parts of flour and butter. The topping would stick to the cake and the crumb topping is softer when made with equal parts flour and butter. Two heads are better than one and many hands do make light work!

Lemon Cream Cheese Pie

1 C sugar	3 T butter
½ C cornstarch	1 can sweetened condensed milk
2 ½ C cold water	1 – 8 oz pkg cream cheese
3 egg yolks	1 small box instant lemon
⅔ C lemon juice	pudding mix
2 graham cracker crusts	⅛ t salt

In a saucepan, combine sugar, cornstarch, and water. Cook over medium heat until thick and clear. Temper egg whites with mixture and add yolks into saucepan. Bring to boil and cook for 1 minute. Remove from heat; add 1/3 C lemon juice, salt, and butter. Cool. Mix 1/3 C lemon juice, sweetened condensed milk, and cream cheese until smooth. Stir into cooled lemon mixture and pour into prepared pie shells. Chill until set.

Sistersfamilyrecipes@gmail.com

Vanilla Cream Pie

This basic cream filling can be modified into coconut cream, chocolate cream, banana cream, butterscotch cream, or used in any recipe that calls for prepared vanilla pudding (like the poppy seed cake recipe).

¾ C sugar	3 T cornstarch
¼ t salt	2 C milk
3 egg yolks beaten	2 T butter
1 t vanilla	1 – 9" baked pastry shell

In saucepan, combine sugar, cornstarch, and salt; gradually stir in milk. Cook and stir over medium heat until bubbly. Cook and stir 2 minutes longer. Remove from heat. Temper egg yolks and add to saucepan; cook 2 minutes more. Remove from heat. Add butter and vanilla. Pour into cooked, cooled pie shell. Cover with plastic wrap and cool completely.

Chocolate Cream: increase sugar to 1 C and add 2 oz chocolate
Banana Cream: add 3 bananas sliced
Butterscotch Cream: substitute brown sugar for sugar and increase butter to 3 T
Coconut Cream: add 1 C toasted coconut

French Silk Pie

1 baked pie crust	⅔ c sugar
2 eggs	2 – 1 ounce unsweetened chocolate, melted
1 tsp vanilla extract	⅓ c. butter, softened
⅔ c. heavy whipping cream	2 tsp. powdered sugar
Whipped Cream and Chocolate curls	

In a small saucepan, combine sugar and eggs until well blended. Cook over low heat, stirring constantly, until mixture reaches 160 and coats and the back of a metal spoon. Remove from the heat. Stir in chocolate and vanilla until smooth. Cool to lukewarm (90 degrees), stirring occasionally. In a small bowl, cream butter until light and fluffy. Add cooled chocolate mixture; beat on high speed for 5 minutes or until light and fluffy. In another large bowl, beat cream until it begins to thicken. Add confectioners' sugar; beat until stiff peaks form. Fold into chocolate mixture. Pour into crust. Chill for at least 6 hours before serving. Garnish with whipped cream and chocolate curls if desired. Refrigerate leftovers.

⤤⤤

It is always surprising to run into someone who cooks who has not made a cream pie from scratch. If you find yourself in that category, try making a cream pie from scratch. You won't believe the difference. We love the convenience of using mixes and boxed pudding mixes to help save time and create richness in some recipes, but you won't believe the difference pudding and pie fillings from scratch can make. There is no substitute.

Peach Cobbler or Pie Filling – Frozen Fresh
This recipe is from Lori Andes it is great to use when you are sick of making peach jam and you still have peaches left. It is quick and easy and is sooo yummy.

8 C. Peaches – peeled and sliced 1 T. Lemon juice
2 C. sugar   ½ C. Flour
1 tsp cinnamon
Mix together and put in a Zip Freezer bag and freeze until ready to use.

Pumpkin Cream Cheese Pie
Cream together and spread into unbaked pie shell:
8 oz cream cheese softened   ¼ C sugar
½ t vanilla   1 egg

Mix:
1 ¼ C canned pumpkin   ½ C sugar
1 ½ t cinnamon   ¼ t ginger
¼ t nutmeg   dash salt
1 C condensed milk   2 eggs

Pour over cream cheese mixture. Bake at 350 for 65 to 70 minutes.

Chocolate Mousse Pie
Crust:
3 C chocolate wafer crumbs   ½ C butter melted
Filling:
1 lb semi-sweet chocolate   6 T powdered sugar
2 eggs   4 egg whites
4 egg yolks   2 C whipping cream

Combine cookie crumbs and butter. Press into a springform pan. Refrigerate for 30 minutes

Melt chocolate in double boiler. Let cool. Add whole eggs and mix well. Add 4 egg yolks and mix well. Whip cream and powdered sugar until soft peak stage. Beat 4 egg whites to soft peak stage. Fold whipped cream and egg whites into chocolate mixture. Pour into crust and chill overnight.

Lemon Meringue Pie

Crust:

½ C soft butter	1 dash salt
1 C flour	⅛ t almond extract
2 T sugar	

Mix ingredients and press into 9" pie plate. Bake at 350 for 25 minutes.

Filling:

7 t cornstarch	1 T grated lemon peel
1 ½ C sugar	½ C lemon juice
¼ t salt	3 egg whites
1 ½ C hot water	¼ t cream of tartar
3 egg yolks, beaten	6 T sugar
2 T butter	

Mix cornstarch, sugar, and salt in saucepan. Gradually stir in water. Cook over heat until very thick and clear (about 10 minutes). Remove from heat. Stir in ½ C hot mixture to egg yolks to temper. Add back into saucepan. Cook on low heat 2 to 3 more minutes. Remove from heat; stir in butter. Add peel and juice. Mix until smooth. Pour into pie shell; cool 1 hour. Top with meringue making sure to seal all edges. Bake at 350 for 15 minutes.

Meringue:

3 egg whites	½ t vanilla
¼ t cream of tartar	6 T sugar

Beat egg whites, vanilla, and cream of tartar until soft peak stage. Gradually add sugar until stiff peak stage.

Meringue Shells

4 egg whites, room temperature
½ tsp. cream of tartar
1 c. sugar

Step 1. Beat egg whites at high speed until soft peaks form. At the soft peak stage, egg whites will curl down when beaters are lifted. Then, gradually add sugar, 1 T. at a time, beating continually until the sugar is completely dissolved.

Step 2. Continue beating until stiff peaks form. At this stage, the egg whites will remain upright when the beaters are lifted.

Step 3. Line a cookie sheet with parchment paper or brown paper. Spoon or pipe the meringue into tarts or desired shapes.

Step 4. Heat oven to 275. Bake shells for 35 minutes. For softer meringues, remove pan from oven immediately. Cool on wire rack. For dry crisp meringues, turn oven off and leave meringues in oven with door closed for 2 hours or overnight.

Step 5. Carefully remove meringues from parchment; place on serving plates. Just before serving, spoon filling into center of each meringue. Makes 6 tartlets.

Meringue Tips

Eggs will separate best when cold from the refrigerator. To avoid getting any yolk in bowl of whites, separate each egg into a small bowl, and then combine with other separated whites and yolks.

To beat egg whites to highest volume:

1) Bring whites to room temperature by setting the bowl of whites into a large bowl of very warm water and stirring gently for a few minutes.

2) Avoid any fat, which reduces foaming action. Make sure the whites contain no specks of yolk and that the bowl and beaters are free of any oil or fat residue. Avoid using plastic bowls because they tent to retain fat.

Cream of tartar, salt, lemon juice or vinegar may be added to increase the stability of beaten egg whites.

Sugar also increases the stability but decreases the volume; therefore it is added gradually during the latter part of beating after the egg whites form soft peaks.

Add sugar gradually while beating continuously until the sugar is completely dissolved and stiff glossy peaks form.

Eggshell fragments that accidentally fall into egg mixtures can be removed using another piece of eggshell.

Humid weather can cause meringues to become soft and sticky.

Store baked dessert meringues in an airtight container at room temperature up to 2 days or freeze them up to 1 month.

Pecan Tart Filling

¾ C corn syrup   ½ C sugar
¼ C brown sugar   3 large eggs
2 T butter (browned)   1 C pecans

Beat all ingredients together except nuts for 3 minutes. Stir in nuts. Bake in pastry lined tart pan (I use the pat in crust above for this recipe.) Bake at 375 for ½ hour. I like to serve caramel sauce over tart slices.

Mini Pecan Tarts

Dough:
½ C butter softened   3 oz cream cheese softened
1 C flour

Cream butter and cheese together until smooth. Add flour. Chill for one hour or overnight. Shape into 1-inch balls and press into mini muffin pans.

Filling:
2 T butter melted   ¾ C brown sugar packed
1 egg   1 t vanilla
1 ½ C chopped pecans

Beat all ingredients until well blended. Fill prepared shells with about 1 T of pecan filling. Bake at 350 for about 20-25 minutes. Makes about 24 tarts.

Lindsay's Favorite Tarts

Tarts:
1 pkg Sugar Cookie mix

Filling:
1 8 ounce package softened cream cheese
1 14 ounce can sweetened condensed milk
⅓ C freshly squeezed lemon juice
zest of one lemon
any combination of berries and kiwi to garnish

Make sugar cookie recipe. Put a small walnut size into the center of each small muffin tin. No need to spray pan. Bake until light brown as recipe indicates. When you remove from oven insert the end of an ice cream scoop (I use my pampered chef pizza cutter) to make an indention/cup in the middle of each tart. Only press down about ¾ to the bottom of the cookie. Let cool. Remove from pan. Fill pastry bag with filling mix and fill the tarts. Add garnish. Serve or chill.

Cheesecake

Best ever!

There are a million ways to customize this basic cheesecake recipe. Start with this base and add fruits, candies, sauces, or cookies to make whatever sounds good. The crust can also be customized to match the filling. Try using ginger snaps with caramel and apple mixed in the filling, chocolate cream filled cookies for cookies and cream filling, or vanilla flavored wafer cookies. The possibilities are endless.

Graham Cracker Crust:

1 ¾ C graham cracker crumbs   ¼ C sugar
   (about 1 pkg)
6 T softened butter

Blend and press into greased, 9" springform pan. Place in refrigerator while making filling.

Basic Filling:
All ingredients work best at room temperature.
4 eggs   1 ¼ C sugar
3 ½ T cornstarch   1 t vanilla
4 – 8 oz. pks cream cheese   1 pint sour cream
⅛ C milk

Beat all ingredients 20 minutes. Pour into springform pan with crust mixture. Bake 1 hour at 350. Set a pan of hot water on the shelf below cheesecake in oven while baking. Turn oven heat off and leave door cracked open for another hour. Cool and refrigerate. Cheesecake is best enjoyed when baked the day before eating.

꙳

Our sister Marti included a special note with this recipe. "Valayne, I beg to differ with you because this is the best cheesecake ever and it never fails. So you better include it in the book also." This recipe is not bad, but maybe you should make both and then decide which one you like the best. We all love to cook and are passionate about the things we make. We all have our favorites and have added our own touches to the recipes we make.

The Truly Best Ever Cheese Cake

Crust:
1 ½ c. graham cracker crumbs
¼ c. sugar
⅓ c. melted butter
Mix ingredients with a fork and press into a 9" spring form pan.

Filling:
2 pkgs. 8 oz cream cheese (softened)
1 can Eagle Brand sweetened condensed milk
3 eggs
¼ c. lemon juice
Beat cream cheese until smooth; add Eagle Brand, mix well. Add eggs one at a time, make sure it is well blended after each egg. Add lemon juice and mix well. Pour over crust and bake 45-50 minutes at 325.

Topping:
8 oz sour cream
½ C sugar
1 tsp vanilla
Stir all ingredients together and spread over warm cheesecake. Bake an additional 5 minutes. Place in the refrigerator until chilled.

Key Lime Cheesecake

10 T butter, melted	4 T sugar
2 C graham cracker crumbs	

Combine together and press into the bottom of a 9 inch spring-form pan. Set aside.

1 ¼ C sugar	1 envelope unflavored gelatin
1 C key lime juice	4 eggs
2 egg yolks	1 lb cream cheese
2 T grated lime zest	2 egg whites at room temperature
Pinch of salt	Sweetened whipped cream (optional)

Dissolve the gelatin and lime juice over medium heat for about 5 minutes. Add sugar, eggs, egg yolks, and lime zest. Cook until mixture thickens and is pudding like – about 7 minutes. Remove from heat.

Cream cheese until smooth. Add lime gelatin mixture and beat until smooth. Remove the mixture and turn into a bowl. Cool completely. Cover with plastic and place in refrigerator. Stir every 10 minutes until chilled.

Whip egg whites and mix in ¼ C sugar until stiff peaks form. Fold into the chilled cheese mixture. Cover with plastic wrap and chill until set – about 3 hours. Spread with topping and chill another hour. Serve at room temperature with whipped cream.

Topping:

8 oz sour cream	½ C sugar
½ C water	Zest of 4 limes
1 tsp vanilla	

Boil water and sugar together to make a simple syrup. Add zest. Simmer for one minute and let cool. Cream softened cheese and add syrup and vanilla and spread over warm cheesecake.

Sistersfamilyrecipes@gmail.com

Mini Cheesecakes

2 – 8 oz cream cheese	1 t vanilla
¾ C sugar	Vanilla Wafer cookies
2 eggs	1 T lemon juice
Canned Cherry Pie Filling + ½ t almond extract	

Line muffin tins with paper liners. Place one cookie in the bottom of each muffin cup. Beat cream cheese and sugar until smooth; add vanilla, eggs, and lemon juice. Spoon mixture into muffin cups 2/3 full. Bake at 350 for 15 – 20 minutes. Cool and top with a spoonful of cherry pie filling.

Black Forest Cheesecake Squares

¼ C oil	1 pkg. Pillsbury Plus Fudge Marble or Fudge Swirl
3 eggs	Cake Mix
½ C sugar	3 (8 oz.) pkg. cream cheese, softened
½ C sour cream	½ C whipping cream

Topping:
1 (21 oz.) can cherry fruit pie filling
½ t almond flavoring

Heat oven to 350 degrees. Grease 13x9 pan. Reserve 1 cup dry cake mix and swirl pouch; set aside. In large bowl, combine remaining cake mix, oil and 1 egg at low speed until dough forms. Press in bottom and 1 inch up sides of greased pan. Bake at 350 for 8 minutes.

In large bowl, beat cream cheese until smooth and creamy. Add 2 eggs, 1 at a time, beating well after each addition. Blend in reserved 1 cup cake mix and remaining cheesecake ingredients at low speed; beat 3 minutes at medium speed until creamy. Reserve 2 cups of cheese mixture. Spoon remaining cheese mixture over base. Add reserved swirl pouch to reserved cheese mixture; blend well. Spoon chocolate mixture evenly over cheese mixture.

Bake at 350 for 30 to 40 minutes until edges are set and center is almost set. Run sharp knife around sides of pan. Cool to room temperature on wire rack.

Stir almond flavoring into pie filling. Spoon evenly over top of cheesecake; refrigerate several hours or overnight before serving.

Pumpkin Pie Cake

This quick and easy cake is a great dessert to take anywhere.

4 eggs	1 ½ C sugar
1 – 16 oz pumpkin pie filling	1 – 13 oz can evaporated milk
2 t pumpkin pie spice	1 box yellow cake mix
¾ t salt	2 sticks butter melted
1 C chopped pecans	

Mix all ingredients together except butter, cake mix, and pecans. Place in 13 X 9 inch baking dish. Sprinkle dry cake mix and nuts on top. Pour melted butter over cake mix and nuts. Bake 90 minutes at 350.

ം∽ക

Our little sister Jana made pumpkin rolls with her youth group as a fundraising project at Christmas time for several years. We don't know how many hundreds of these she has made, but she still loves them and they are a great make-ahead dessert. Pumpkin Rolls are a delicious dessert to keep or give as a gift. You could also make a few hundred and sell them as a fundraiser! The great thing about them is you can make several of these up in advance and keep them in the freezer until you need a fabulous dessert. Take the Roll out of the freezer, dust with a little confectioner's sugar, slice and serve.

Pumpkin Rolls

3 eggs	2 t cinnamon
1 C sugar	1 t ginger
1 t lemon juice	½ t nutmeg
¾ C flour	½ t salt
1 t baking powder	1 C chopped nuts
⅔ C pumpkin	

Beat eggs for 5 minutes until light and fluffy. Mix in the rest of the ingredients and bake in a greased jellyroll pan lined with greased waxed paper or parchment paper. The waxed paper or parchment paper is a must. Bake at 350 for 15 minutes. While baking prepare a clean kitchen towel by sprinkling it liberally with powdered sugar. Turn baked cake onto dusted kitchen towel, remove paper from top, and roll up loosely in kitchen towel. Cool completely.

Filling:

½ C + 2 T powdered sugar	4 t butter softened
1 – 8 oz cream cheese softened	1 t vanilla

Cream cheese and sugar until smooth and creamy. Add butter and vanilla. Spread filling into cooled cake you have unrolled. Roll back up, wrap in plastic wrap and chill or freeze until ready to serve.

Poppy Seed Cake

This is Tom's favorite cake. Valayne usually makes it for his birthday. His mom gave us the recipe and we have changed it a little. Her recipe calls for raisins in the filling. We are not huge raisin fans. We call them ticks – sorry, they look a little like ticks! Dried currents are a great substitute.

Sweet dough (you can use this dough for cinnamon rolls too):

3 ½ - 4 C. flour	¼ C shortening
1 pkg dry yeast	1 t salt
1 C milk warmed	2 eggs
¼ C sugar	

Mix flour and yeast together. Add warm milk, shortening, and sugar. Mix well. Add eggs and salt. Knead and shape into soft dough ball. Let rise for 1 hour. Punch down and roll into a rectangle about ½" thick. Christa says that the best recipes are by weight. She uses 1lb of flour for her sweet dough.

Filling:
One recipe of vanilla pie filling either homemade from above recipes or from a box. Homemade always tastes better, but we don't always have time for that.

½ C sugar   4 oz ground almonds (grind in food processor or
1 C poppy seeds ground to paste spice grinder)
(this is available canned, but isn't as good)

Spread on rolled dough and roll up along widest end. Let rise 30-60 minutes. Brush top of roll with warm water. Top with our favorite streusel topping (recipe above) and bake at 325 for 60-80 minutes. Top with glaze of powdered sugar and milk after baking.

Macadamia Nut Cake

We got this great recipe from our friend Sue Smith. She uses it for all her wedding cakes. It is a great tasting cake that frosts beautifully. It has been the star at many of our wedding celebrations. This recipe makes two round layers but is easily doubled or tripled.

1 C buttermilk	5 eggs (separated)
1 t soda	2 cubes butter
1 C sugar	2 C flour
1 C macadamia nuts	1 C coconut

Mix milk, egg yolks (save egg whites), and soda; set aside. Cream butter and sugar until light and smooth. Place nuts and flour in the food processor and process until nuts are powdered. Beat egg whites until stiff peak. Add milk mixture to creamed butter and sugar. Add dry ingredients to milk mixture. Fold in egg whites and coconut. Pour into cake pans. Bake at 350 until done.

Cindy's Carrot Cake

Mix together:

2 t. baking soda	2 C flour
2 C sugar	2 t cinnamon
1 t salt	

Stir in:

¾ buttermilk	¼ C oil
2 t vanilla	3 beaten eggs

Mix in:

7 oz coconut	1 C crushed, drained pineapple
½ C golden raisins	1 C nuts
2 C grated, raw carrots	

Bake in greased and floured 13 X 9 pan at 350 for 50 minutes. Frost with cream cheese icing when completely cooled.

Cream Cheese Icing

8 oz cream cheese softened	1 stick softened butter
1 t vanilla	1 box powdered sugar

Cream together until smooth and spreadable.

Flourless Chocolate Cake

4 T cocoa powder	1 cube butter
9 large eggs (separated)	¾ C sugar
2 C heavy cream	powdered sugar

Melt butter and cocoa powder together in small saucepan on medium heat. Beat together egg yolks and sugar until light and creamy. Slowly whisk in chocolate mixture. Beat egg whites until stiff peak stage. Fold into the chocolate mixture. Pour into buttered, 9-inch springform pan. Bake in preheated 350 degree oven for 20 – 25 minutes. Cool 10 minutes and remove from pan. Sprinkle with powdered sugar. Top with whipped cream when serving.

Spice Cake

2 C flour	½ t nutmeg
1 ½ C brown sugar packed	¼ C butter
1 ¼ t soda	¼ C shortening
1 t baking powder	2 eggs
½ t salt	1 C sour cream
2 t cinnamon	½ C water
¾ t ground cloves	½ C nuts chopped

Cream butter, shortening, and sugar until smooth and creamy. Add sour cream, eggs, and water. Mix dry ingredients and pour into greased and floured pans. Frost with cream cheese icing with maple flavoring added or caramel icing below.

Zeke's Mom's Caramel Icing

½ C melted butter	1 C packed Brown sugar

Boil over medium heat for two minutes then add ¼ C milk and bring to boil again. Remove from heat and cool until warm. Gradually add 1 ½ - 2 C powdered sugar and a pinch of salt. Let cool and frost cake.

Sistersfamilyrecipes@gmail.com

Sour Cream Chocolate Cake
2 C flour
2 C sugar
1 C water
¾ C sour cream
¼ C shortening
4 oz melted chocolate

1 ¼ t baking soda
1 t salt
1 t vanilla
2 eggs
½ t baking powder

Heat oven to 350. Grease and flour a 13 X 9 pan. Mix all ingredients for 2 minutes on low. Pour into pan and bake 40 – 45 minutes. Frost with sour Cream Chocolate icing when cool.

Sour Cream Chocolate Icing
⅓ C butter softened
3 oz melted unsweetened chocolate
2 t vanilla

3 C powdered sugar
½ C sour cream

Mix butter and cooled chocolate well. Blend in sugar, sour cream, and vanilla. Beat until frosting is smooth and spreadable. Frost completely cooled cake.

Swedish Apple Cake
Cream together:

½ C butter
2 large eggs

2 C sugar

Add to above:

2 C flour
2 tsp. soda
2 tsp. cinnamon

½ tsp. salt
4 c. shredded (grated) granny smith apples

Grease and flour 9 x 13 inch pan. Pour mixture into pan and sprinkle with 1/2 - 1/4 cup chopped pecans. Bake at 350 degrees.

Caramel Sauce:
½ C butter
½ C half & half

1 C brown sugar
1 tsp. vanilla

Add together. Cook and stir until boiling. When cake is done, pour over top.

German Chocolate Cake Frosting

1 C sugar	½ C butter
3 egg yolks	1 t vanilla
1 C evaporated milk	

Mix ingredients in medium saucepan and heat until thickened and bubbly (about 12 minutes). Add 1 1/3 C coconut and 1 C chopped nuts. Beat until thick enough to spread.

Seven Minute Frosting

Our friend Sue Smith makes this and frosts a chocolate cake directly from the oven. We call it "Hot Chocolate Cake" there is nothing like it!

2 egg whites	¼ tsp cream of tartar
¾ c. sugar	dash of salt
⅓ c. light corn syrup	1 tsp vanilla extract
3 T. water	

Combine all ingredients except vanilla in a metal bowl placed over a pan of boiling water or a double boiler. Cook over low heat, beating constantly with a portable electric mixer until frosting is fluffy and stands in peaks, about 7 minutes.

Remove from heat, and fold in vanilla. Frost a Chocolate cake that is still hot from the oven. It is fabulous.

Blueberry Crumb Cake

This is also a great basic vanilla cake recipe that can be used as the base for any cake. Add nuts, fruits, fillings, and frost with icing of just about any kind. This blueberry cake makes a great breakfast cake or dessert cake.

Cake:

6 T butter (3/4 stick)	¾ C sugar
2 extra-large eggs	1 t vanilla
⅔ C sour Cream	1 ¼ C all-purpose flour
1 t baking powder	¼ t baking soda
½ t salt	1 C fresh blueberries

Cream butter and sugar for 4 – 5 minutes until light and creamy. Add eggs one at a time. Add sour cream and mix until smooth. Mix in dry ingredients until well blended. Stir in blueberries. Pour batter into buttered, 9- inch cake pan. Top with streusel topping. Bake at 350 for 40 – 50 minutes or until toothpick comes out clean.

Streusel Topping

¼ C sugar	⅓ C packed brown sugar
1 stick butter melted	1 ⅓ C flour

Mix flour and sugars together then blend in butter. Mix with a fork and crumble over cake batter.

Cathy's Rum Cake

1 box Yellow Cake mix	¼ C powdered sugar
2 – 4 oz boxes vanilla pudding	1 – 8 oz whipped topping thawed
2 C milk (separated)	coconut
1 – 8 oz cream cheese	canned fruit, drained
½ t rum flavoring	

Follow directions on cake mix and bake in cookie sheet. Cool and set aside. Mix 1 box of pudding, 1 C milk and softened cream cheese until smooth. Spread over cooled cake. Spread drained fruit over cheese layer. Mix 1 box of pudding, 1 C milk, powdered sugar and rum flavoring; beat until smooth. Fold in whipped topping and spread over fruit layer. Chill until set.

German Chocolate Upside-down Cake

1 ½ C Coconut	1 ½ C Pecans
Swiss Chocolate Cake mix	8 oz Cream cheese
½ C butter (melted)	4 C Powdered Sugar

Grease and Flour 9 x 13 pan. Sprinkle coconut and flour in bottom of pan. Make cake according to directions pour over nuts and coconut. Beat cream cheese and butter, add powdered sugar. With a large spoon drop mixture in blobs on cake. Bake at 350 degrees for 45 – 50 minutes. Let cool, then invert.

Lemon Cake

1 box lemon cake mix	1 small box lemon gelatin
¾ C water	¾ C oil
4 eggs	1 tsp lemon juice

Bake in greased 13x9 at 325 for 30 min.

Glaze:
5 T. lemon juice
2 tsp butter
2 C powdered sugar

❧❧

Valayne first ate this cake at a Bunko night. A friend of hers brought this cake to share with the group as they talked about their kids, their challenges, and solved all their problems just by talking together with other moms. This dessert is quick and easy and you can take it anywhere easily. Just baking it can make you smile. That wonderful smell of pumpkin can warm up any chilly fall day or night. There is something about baking pumpkin that just says home and fall – two of the greatest things on earth.

Pumpkin Dump Cake

1 yellow cake mix (butter cake)- save 1 C for topping
½ C butter
1 egg

Press into 9x13 sprayed with non-stick cooking spray.

Filling:

29 oz. can pumpkin	1 can evaporated milk
4 eggs, slightly beaten	2 tsp cinnamon
½ tsp cloves	1 ½ C sugar
1 t. salt	1 t. ginger

Pour over unbaked crust.

Topping:

1 C reserved cake mix	½ c. sugar
1 tsp cinnamon	¼ C butter, softened

Sprinkle over filling. Bake at 350 for 60-70 min.
Serve with dollop of French vanilla cool whip.

Black Bottom Cupcakes

Mix and set aside:

8 oz. cream cheese	⅓ C sugar
6 oz chocolate chips	1 egg
⅛ tsp salt	

Combine and set aside:
½ c. nuts, chopped
½ c. sugar

Combine and mix:

1 ½ C flour	¼ C cocoa
⅓ C oil	1 t. vanilla
1 t. baking soda,	1 C sugar
½ t. salt	1 t. vinegar
1 C water	

Spray muffin tins with non-stick spray. Fill cupcakes 1/3 full with cake mixture. Top with spoonful of cream cheese mixture. Sprinkle with nut mixture.
Bake at 350 degrees for 30 min.

Oatmeal Chocolate Chip Cake

This recipe is from Aunt Sylvia and Marti uses it for wedding cake. She uses multiple recipes of it and puts all of the chips and nuts into the cake and none on top. Moist and delicious!

1 ¾ C boiling water	1 ¾ C flour
1 C uncooked oatmeal	1 t baking soda
1 C packed brown sugar	½ t salt
1 C sugar	4 T cocoa powder
1 cube butter	1- 12 oz chocolate chips
3 eggs	½ C nuts

Pour boiling water over oatmeal add butter and let stand 10 minutes. Add brown and white sugar. Mix well, add eggs, and mix well. Add dry ingredients mix well; stir in ½ pkg chocolate chips. Pour batter into a well greased and floured 9x13 pan. Sprinkle nuts and remaining chocolate chips on top. Bake in preheated oven at 350 degrees for 40 minutes.

Strawberry Refrigerator Cake

Strawberry Cake Mix
1 C milk
2 C cool whip
Fresh strawberries, opt.

2 (10 oz) pkgs sweetened, frozen sliced
    strawberries, thawed.
1 pkg. (4-serving size) vanilla instant pudding

Prepare cake following package directions. Cool. Poke holes 1 inch apart in top of cake using handle from a wooden spoon. Puree thawed strawberries with juice in blender. Spoon evenly over top of cake allowing mixture to soak into holes.

For topping, prepare pudding mix using 1 c. milk. Fold cool whip into pudding mixture. Spread over cake. Garnish with fresh strawberries. Refrigerate at least 4 hours.

Harvest Pumpkin Brownie with Caramel Sauce

Beat together:
16 oz can pumpkin
¾ C oil

4 eggs
2 t vanilla

Add:
2 C flour
1 T pumpkin pie spice
2 t cinnamon
½ t salt

2 C sugar
2 t baking powder
1 t baking soda

Pour into greased jellyroll pan. Bake at 350 for 20-25 min.

Caramel Sauce:
½ C butter
2 T light corn syrup
Pecans, chopped

1 ¼ C brown sugar
½ C whipping cream

Melt butter. Stir in sugar and syrup. Boil until sugar is dissolved. Stir in whipping cream and return to boil. Add chopped pecans. Serve over vanilla ice cream and Harvest Pumpkin Brownie.

જસ્જી

This cake recipe should be added as a tier on the food pyramid. It is one of the staples of life. If you need to bring a dessert for a crowd somewhere or need a quick dessert for a crowd – and there always seems to be a crowd when we gather or go anywhere – this is your recipe. It is quick, easy, and good. The batter is also one of the best ever. Just try not to lick the bowl! This recipe is difficult to ruin, although Kailee and Demie were assigned to make it for a family gathering and it was a disaster. That may be due more to talking and having too much fun while baking together and not paying attention to who is adding what! We are not sure what they did, but it is a sure bet they did more talking than following the recipe. Don't let baking with a friend distract you!

Texas Sheet Cake Perfected

Martie has made this recipe the most – because she is the oldest! She feels she finally perfected this recipe on May 3, 2009 the best Texas Sheet Cake recipe ever. Our original recipe is from an old church cookbook, but it needed some tweaking.

2 C flour	1 t vanilla
2 C sugar	2 cubes butter
1 ½ t baking soda	½ C sour cream
2 eggs	4 T cocoa powder
1 C water	

In a large bowl, mix flour, sugar and baking soda. In a small bowl, whisk together eggs, water and vanilla. Add to the dry ingredients and mix with a hand mixer until blended. In a medium saucepan over medium heat; melt butter, sour cream and cocoa, heat just until butter melts and everything is stirred together. Add to mixture in bowl; mix until blended. Batter will be thin. Pour into a greased cookie sheet type pan with high sides. Bake at 350 degrees for 23 – 27 minutes.

Frosting –

½ C sour cream	1 t vanilla
2 T cocoa	4 ½ C powdered sugar
1 cube butter	1 C chopped and toasted almonds

Melt sour cream, cocoa and butter in the medium saucepan (used previously), to a bubbly boil. Remove from heat and with a hand mixer, add powdered sugar and vanilla, mix until smooth and creamy. Add nuts. Frost while cake is hot.

* There is a variation to this great cake that is as good as the original. Substitute one mashed banana for the cocoa and frost with cream cheese frosting. Our friend Linda Wisheart gave us this idea. This variation is surprisingly delicious.

Chocolate Cupcakes with Cream Cheese Filling
Cake:

3 C flour

2 C sugar

½ t salt

½ C cocoa

2 t soda

Mix together.

Add:

2 C water

⅔ C oil

2 T vinegar

2 t vanilla

Fill cupcake papers half full and add a teaspoon of cheese filling on top.

Cheese filling:

1 – 8oz pkg. cream cheese

½ C sugar

1 egg

Mix together.

Bake at 350 degrees for 30 minutes. Cool. Frost cupcakes with Cream Cheese Frosting.

Sistersfamilyrecipes@gmail.com

Tres Leches Cake

1 ¼ C cake flour	1 t baking powder
¼ t salt	1 C sugar
⅓ C oil	5 eggs
1 t vanilla	½ C milk

Combine flour, baking powder and salt. In a separate bowl, combine the oil, sugar and vanilla. Add the eggs, one at a time until well combined. Stir in the milk, and then gently fold in the flour mixture a little at a time. Pour batter into a greased 9x13 pan and bake at 325 degrees for 30-40 minutes or until it feels firm and an inserted toothpick come out clean. Let cake cool to room temperature. Pierce cake with a fork 20-30 times. Let it cool for an additional 2-3 hours.

Whisk together:
1 C milk	1 C sweetened condensed milk
1 C heavy cream	1 t rum flavoring

Slowly pour over cooled cake. Refrigerate for 1 hour. Then frost with whipped cream frosting.

Frosting:
¾ c. cream	1 tsp. vanilla
¼ c. sugar	

Put all ingredients in a mixing bowl. Beat until peaks form. Spread over the cake. Refrigerate until ready to serve.

Gelatin Cake

1 Lemon Cake mix	1 small box lime gelatin
1 C hot water	

Make cake according to directions on box in 9 X 13 cake pan. While cake is baking, dissolve gelatin in hot water. Remove cake from oven and cool slightly. Poke hole in cake with fork and pour gelatin mixture evenly over cake. Chill. Frost with sweetened whipped cream flavored with lemon. This recipe can be changed by varying the flavor of gelatin and flavor of cake used. It works equally well with a yellow cake. It is a yummy and cool dessert. This dessert tastes great on a hot summer day. Store leftover cake in the refrigerator.

Amaretto Cake with Cinnamon Swirl

1 C sliced almonds	1 T cinnamon
3 T almond paste	1 White cake mix
1 – 8oz carton sour cream	1 small box white chocolate instant pudding
4 eggs lightly beaten	½ C cooking oil
1 t almond extract + ½ c. water	

Preheat oven to 350 degrees. Generously grease 10" (12 cup) fluted tube pan. In food processor combine almonds and cinnamon, process until nuts are finely chopped. Coat bottom and sides of pan with 1/3 the mixture. Add almond paste to remaining mixture in processor. Process until combined.

In large mixing bowl combine cake and pudding mixes, sour cream, eggs, ½ c. water, oil and almond and water mixture. Beat with mixer on low speed to combine. Beat on medium speed 2 minutes, scraping bowl as needed. Spoon half the batter into pan. Evenly sprinkle cinnamon almond paste mixture over batter. Spoon remaining batter on cinnamon mixture.

Bake about 55 minutes or until wooden pick inserted near center comes out clean. Cool in pan 10 minutes. Remove from pan. Place on rack over waxed paper. Using wooden skewer, poke several holes in cake. Prepare Glaze: spoon over cake.

Glaze:

⅓ C milk	2 T butter
1 ½ C powdered sugar	½ t almond extract

Whisk together; pour over cake.

World's Best Brownies

1 C melted margarine	1 ½ C flour
2 C sugar	1 t vanilla
½ C cocoa powder	4 eggs

Mix sugar, cocoa powder, and flour; add melted margarine. Mix in eggs one at a time with a fork. Do not over mix. Add vanilla. Bake at 350 degrees for 25 minutes.

Sistersfamilyrecipes@gmail.com

Blondies
½ C shortening
2 C brown sugar
2 t vanilla
1 ½ C flour

2 eggs
2 t baking powder
¼ t salt

Melt shortening in large saucepan; add remaining ingredients. Spread into a 9x13 greased pan. Bake at 350 degrees for 25 – 30 minutes.

Zebra Brownies
We like them because they are fast, in case you need a dessert in a hurry. These are also very delicious! Dense, sweet, and creamy.

Brownies:
Use a box mix of your choice for a 9 x 13 pan. Mix following the package directions.

Filling:
¼ C sugar
½ t vanilla

1 (8oz) pkg. cream cheese, softened
1 egg

Heat oven to 350 degrees. Grease or spray bottom only of a 13x9 pan. In small bowl blend all filling ingredients; beat 1 minute. Set aside. In large bowl make the brownies according to the box directions. Spread half of the batter in prepared pan. Pour cream cheese mixture over batter, spreading to cover. Place spoonfuls of remaining batter on top of cream cheese. Marble by pulling knife through batter in wide curves. Bake for 30 to 35 minutes. Do not over bake. Cool: for ease in cutting refrigerate at least 1 hour. Then cut with a plastic knife.

Rocky Road Fudge Bars

Base

½ C butter	3 T Cocoa powder
1 C flour	1 C sugar
1 t baking powder	1 t vanilla

2 eggs

¾ c. chopped nuts (we like walnuts or toasted almonds)

Filling:

¼ C butter softened	1 (8 oz.) pkg. cream cheese softened, reserving 2 oz for frosting.
½ C sugar	
½ t vanilla	2 T flour
¼ C chopped nuts	1 egg

Frosting:

2 C miniature marshmallows	¼ C butter
¼ C milk	3 T cocoa
2 oz. reserved cream cheese	3 C powdered sugar, sifted
1 t vanilla	

Heat oven to 350 degrees. Grease and flour 13x9 pan. In large saucepan melt ½ c. butter and stir in the cocoa over low heat, stirring until smooth. Add 1 c. flour and remaining base ingredients; mix well. Spread into greased and floured pan.

In small bowl, combine all filling ingredients except ¼ c. nuts. Beat 1 minute at medium speed until smooth and fluffy; stir in nuts. Spread over chocolate mixture.

Bake at 350 degrees for 25 to 35 minutes until toothpick inserted in center comes out clean. Immediately sprinkle marshmallows over top. Return to oven and bake an additional 2 minutes.

Meanwhile, in large saucepan over low heat, combine ¼ c. butter, milk, cocoa and reserved 2 oz. cream cheese; stir until well blended. Remove from heat; stir in powdered sugar and 1 tsp vanilla until smooth. Immediately pour frosting over marshmallows and lightly swirl with knife to marble. Refrigerate until firm.

Sistersfamilyrecipes@gmail.com

Chocolate Mint Brownies

1 C flour
½ C butter, softened
½ t salt
4 eggs

1 t vanilla
1 can chocolate-flavored syrup
1 C sugar

In a large mixing bowl, combine all ingredients. Beat on medium speed for 3 minutes. Pour batter into a greased 9x13 pan. Bake at 350 degrees for 30 minutes. Cool completely.

Filling:
½ C butter, softened
2 C powdered sugar
1 T water

½ t mint extract
3 drops green food coloring

In a large mixing bowl, beat the butter, powdered sugar, water mint, and food coloring until creamy. Spread over cooled brownies. Refrigerate until set.

Topping:
1 pkg. (10 oz) mint chocolate chips
½ C plus 1 T butter cubed

Melt chocolate chips and butter over low heat in a small saucepan. Let cool for 30 minutes, stirring occasionally. Spread over filling. Chill. Cut into squares. Store brownies in refrigerator.

Chocolate Chip Cheesecake Bars

¾ C butter	1 ½ C flour
¾ C sugar	1 t salt
1/3 C packed brown sugar	¾ t baking soda
1 egg	1 ½ C miniature chocolate chips
1 ½ t vanilla	¾ C chopped (pecans or walnuts)

In a mixing bowl, cream butter and sugars. Beat in egg and vanilla. Combine the flour, salt and baking soda; add to the creamed mixture and mix well. Fold in the chocolate chips and nuts. Set aside a third of the dough for topping. Press remaining dough into a greased 9x13 baking pan. Bake at 350 degrees for 8 minutes.

Filling:

2 - 8 oz cream cheese, softened	¾ C sugar
2 eggs	1 t vanilla

In a small mixing bowl, beat cream cheese and sugar until smooth. Add eggs and vanilla; mix well. Spoon filling over crust. Drop teaspoonfuls of reserved dough over filling. Bake at 350 degrees for 35-40 minutes or until golden brown. Cool on a wire rack. Store bars in the refrigerator.

❧❧

One of our Christmas traditions is to make gingerbread houses. Several weeks before Christmas, we make the gingerbread, cut it into house shapes, frost and add all kinds of candies we have collected over the year. Our kids loved this activity. There were no rules, and everyone got to make their own house. Oh, sure, it was a huge mess and sticky frosting gets everywhere, but it was a lot of fun. The houses would be displayed until long after Christmas. Ryan and Preston's houses were usually half eaten before Christmas!

Debbie's Gingerbread

2 ¾ C flour	3 t baking soda
½ t salt	1 t cinnamon
1 t ginger	⅔ C molasses
1 egg	½ C oil
⅛ t ground cloves	⅓ C sugar

Mix ingredients and roll out right in cookie sheet. Bake at 300 degrees for about 30 minutes. Cut into desired shapes while still warm. Cool completely and frost with icing below. Decorate with candy, cereal, and nuts.

Royal Icing

2 egg whites	⅛ t cream of tartar
2 t water	2 ½ to 3 C powdered sugar
Food coloring (optional)	

This icing recipe dries very hard. Beat egg whites, cream of tartar, and water with electric mixer until frothy. Gradually add powdered sugar. Beat until stiff peaks form. Place in plastic zip-seal bag with a tiny part of one corner cut out to use as a piping bag.

New Recipes

~ Cookies ~

⤳⤳⤥

Cookies are one of the secrets to a happy life. A week without cookies is like a week without sunshine. If you haven't smelled cookies that you made baking in your oven, you are missing out on something really great that can't be duplicated. We believe the world would be a better place if everyone made cookies at least once a week. A cookie recipe makes more cookies than you can eat, so they beg you to share them. Bake some cookies and share them and see if it doesn't change your world just a little. A few cookies in a bag with some ribbon can be a prize for a game, a treat for a friend, a gift for a sick neighbor, or a hug for a kid or co-worker. A few cookies on a plate can make someone's day when they come home to find them. Many cookies on a plate can be the start of a great party or the best part of a child's day. One of the best things about making cookies is eating some of the dough. We know what the experts say – don't eat raw eggs or cookie dough. We certainly wouldn't want to encourage anything that would cause someone to get sick, so don't eat raw dough. That said, we have eaten dough and batter of all kinds for more years than we'd like to admit and we have never gotten sick. We have made cookies for the sole purpose of eating the dough! Invite a friend over, gather some kids around, or just get in the kitchen yourself to bake some cookies and change the world.

Gingerbread Cookies

1 C shortening	1 C sugar
1 egg	½ C sour cream
½ C molasses	2 t baking soda (separated)
4 C flour	1 t ground ginger
1 t cinnamon	

Cream together shortening and sugar; beat in egg until well blended. Add sour cream and mix well. Combine molasses and 1 t of baking soda in small bowl then add to creamed mixture. Slowly add flour, one cup at a time mixing well after each addition. Add soda and spices. Chill for 2 hours. Roll out on floured surface to ¼" thick and cut into desired shapes. Bake at 350 degrees for 8 minutes.

No Bake Cookies

Tom's all time favorite! He can seriously smell these being made from 5 miles away. Don't be surprised if he shows up at your door just as they are ready to eat!

2 C Sugar	1 Stick butter or margarine
4 T Cocoa Powder	½ C Milk

Bring to boil in medium saucepan over medium heat. Boil for 1 minute. (this is the crucial part of this simple recipe. You must boil the cookie dough for one minute.) Add ½ C. peanut butter, 1 t. vanilla, and 2 C. instant oats. Mix well and spoon onto waxed paper. Let cool.

Chewy Chocolate Crinkles

¼ C butter	3 T cocoa
¼ C shortening	2 C sifted flour
1 C sugar	1 t baking powdered
⅔ C brown sugar	½ t salt
2 eggs	⅓ C milk
2 t vanilla	½ C walnuts

Cream shortening and sugar; add eggs vanilla and cocoa. Sift dry ingredients together and add alternately with milk. Stir in nuts. Form into 1" balls and roll in powdered sugar. Place on a greased cookie sheet 2-3" apart. Bake at 350 degrees for 12-15 minutes.

Swedish Oatmeal Cookies

¾ C flour	½ C butter
½ C sugar	½ t vanilla
½ C brown sugar	1 egg
½ t salt	1 ½ C oatmeal
½ t baking soda	

Drop spoonfuls on greased cookie sheet bake at 350 degrees for 8 minutes. Remove from oven and place ½ tsp. of filling into center of each cookie and then bake for an additional 6-8 minutes.

Filling:

⅓ C sugar	⅓ C slivered almonds
¼ C butter	¼ t almond extract
1 T light corn syrup	

Place all ingredients in a small saucepan and bring to a boil. Remove from heat.

❧❧

We have tried to combine and condense duplicated recipes to make sure we have one recipe of everything we make and not three or four versions, so you may be wondering why we have included so many chocolate chip cookie recipes. If you are a cookie person, you have a favorite chocolate chip cookies recipe! We couldn't combine these, as they are all different. They all have slightly different tastes and textures. We suggest you try them all. We may not be the best cookie makers, but we love to eat the dough! Cookie recipes don't often double well. The flour needs to be adjusted and they never come out as good when the recipe is doubled. You need to measure carefully when you make cookies – something we have trouble with. We like to just throw things in or measure with our hands; that is not a good idea when making cookies or for most baking recipes.

Karyn, a good friend of Valayne's, is a great cook who makes awesome cookies, but she is a perfect example of why things might taste differently if you don't follow the recipe as written. She asked Valayne for a recipe one day. Valayne asked her later how the recipe turned out and she said it didn't taste as good as when Valayne made it. When asked how she made the cookies, she began recounting her experience by saying, "well I didn't have any of this, so I substituted that, and I didn't have enough of this, so I put in that…" Valayne just started to laugh! If you want it to taste just like the recipe, you have to follow the recipe and measure carefully when you bake.

<u>Chocolate Chip Cookies</u>

Amie and Kirbie got this recipe from a friend Heather Porter and Martie says she has truly never tasted better chocolate chip cookies and she doesn't even like Chocolate Chip cookies. You need to make this in a stand mixer or your arms will get awfully tired!

In a mixer combine:
1 ½ C brown sugar   2 C white sugar

Mix sugars together on medium speed for 4 minutes.

Add to the sugar mixture:
4 sticks butter   3 eggs
2 t Vanilla

Mix sugar, eggs and vanilla on medium-high speed for 4 minutes.

Add dry ingredients:
1 ½ t salt   1 ½ t baking soda
6 C flour
Mix together well. Add 2-4 cups of milk chocolate chips. Roll into balls and then roll in white sugar to coat. Place on greased cookie sheet. Bake at 350 degrees for 11 minutes.

Aunt Sylvia's Chocolate Chip Cookies

1 C shortening	1 C sugar
1 C brown sugar	½ t salt
2 eggs	1 t baking soda
1 t baking powder	2 C flour
2 C Old fashioned Oats	2 t Vanilla
1 C chopped nuts if desired	1 C. coconut if desired
1 ½ C chocolate chips	

Drop by spoonfuls onto cookie sheet. Bake at 350 degrees for 10 to 12 minutes. (Depends on your oven. Check after 10 minutes so cookies are not over done.) Makes 6 dozen.

Macadamia White Chocolate Chip Cookies

1 C butter	3 ½ C flour
1 C salad oil	1 t salt
1 C brown sugar	1 t baking soda
1 C sugar	1 C oatmeal
1 egg	1 C coconut
2 t vanilla	1 C rice cereal
1 t cream of tartar	1 - 12 oz pkg white chocolate chips
1 C toasted macadamia nuts	

Cream together: butter, oil, and sugars; add egg and vanilla. Sift together flour, salt and soda; stir into butter mixture. Add remaining ingredients and stir until blended. Drop by heaping spoonfuls onto a greased cookie sheet and bake at 350 degrees for 12 minutes.

Just Like the Mall Chocolate Chip Cookies

This is the recipe we made all the time for years, until we received cookies from a friend and loved them. We asked for her recipe and she said she just uses the one off the back of the chocolate chip bag! We had quit using that one in favor of this – go figure! That recipe follows this one.

1 C unsalted butter, softened	1 t baking soda
1 C sugar	2 C flour
1 C brown sugar	1 t vanilla
2 eggs	1 chocolate bar, grated
2 ½ C powdered oatmeal	½ t salt
1 t baking powder	1 ½ C nuts, chopped

Cream butter and sugars; add eggs and mix well. Add oatmeal that has been powdered in a blender until fine. Add all other dry ingredients. Add vanilla, chips, chocolate, and nuts. This makes a very stiff dough. Spoon onto cookie sheets and bake at 400 degrees for 8 minutes.

Chocolate Chip Cookies

2 1/4 C all-purpose flour	1 t baking soda
1 t salt	1 C butter, softened
¾ C granulated sugar	¾ C packed brown sugar
1 t vanilla extract	2 large eggs
2 C chocolate chips	1 C chopped nuts

Cream butter and sugar, add flavoring. Add dry ingredients then stir in chips and nuts. Bake at 350 degrees for 10-12 minutes or until lightly golden brown.

Cream Wafers

1 c. soft butter
1/3 c. whipping cream
2 c. flour

Mix thoroughly. Chill 1 hour. Heat oven to 375 degrees. Roll dough 1/8" thick. Cut into 1 ½" rounds. Transfer to waxed paper heavily sprinkled with sugar; turn to coat both sides. Place on ungreased cookie sheet. Prick four times with a fork. Bake 7 – 9 minutes or until slightly puffy. Put two cooled cookies together with filling.

Filling:
¼ C soft butter   1 egg yolk
¾ C powdered sugar   1 t vanilla

Blend thoroughly; spread between two wafer cookies.

Chocolate Cookie Balls

1 Package chocolate cream filled cookies (crushed)
1 – 8oz. Package of cream cheese (softened)
1 t vanilla
¼ C Sugar

Cream cheese, sugar, and vanilla. Stir in crushed cookies. Form into balls. Chill until firm. Melt 1 cup milk chocolate chips in double boiler. Dip balls into chocolate. Place on cookie sheet and chill until set.

Soft Gingersnap Cookies

1 ½ C butter, softened   4 t baking soda
2 C packed brown sugar   2 t cinnamon
2 eggs   2 t ginger
½ C molasses   1 t ground cloves
4 ½ C flour   ½ t salt
Raw sugar

Cream together butter, brown sugar, eggs and molasses. In a separate bowl, combine all remaining ingredients except raw sugar; add to creamed mixture and beat together. Cover bowl and chill in refrigerator for at least 1 hour. Using 1 tablespoon as a measure, roll dough into balls, making about 48 dough balls. Dip tops in raw sugar. Place balls, on greased baking sheets about 3 inches apart. Bake at 350 degrees for 10 to 12 minutes. Immediately remove cookies from baking sheets and cool on wire racks.

Coconut Chews

Crust:

¾ C butter	½ t baking powder
¾ C powdered sugar	½ t salt
1 ½ C flour	½ t vanilla

Heat oven to 350 degrees. Cream butter and sugar. Blend in flour, baking powder, salt and vanilla. Press into a 9x13 pan and bake for 12-15 minutes.

Filling:

2 eggs	1 C nuts (walnuts)
1 C brown sugar	½ C coconut
2 T flour	

Mix all ingredients. Spread over hot baked crust and bake for an additional 20 minutes. While still warm frost.

Orange-Lemon Icing

1 ½ C powdered sugar	2 T butter (melted)
3 T Orange juice	1 T Lemon juice

Wisk together and pour over warm filling.

Peanut Blossom Cookies

1 ¾ C flour	½ C sugar
½ C packed brown sugar	1 t baking soda
½ t salt	½ C shortening
½ C peanut butter	2 T milk
1 t vanilla	1 egg
Sugar to roll cookie balls in	48 unwrapped chocolate kisses

Heat oven to 375 degrees. In large bowl mix cookie ingredients on low speed until a stiff dough forms. Shape into 1" balls and roll in sugar. Place on ungreased cookie sheet. Bake 10-12 minutes. Immediately press into the center of hot cookies 1 candy kiss; remove from cookie sheet and cool until chocolate kiss is firm.

Variation:

1 can sweetened condensed milk	1 t vanilla
¾ C peanut butter	1 egg
2 C baking mix	48 unwrapped chocolate kiss candies.

Follow same directions above.

Chocolate Mint Cookies

¾ C butter   ½ C brown sugar
2 T water   ½ pkg. semi sweet chocolate chips
½ pkg. milk chocolate chips

Combine on medium heat in a saucepan, stir until butter and chocolate is melted.
Turn off heat and Add:
2 eggs   2 ½ C flour
1 ¼ t soda   ½ t salt

Stir until stiff dough forms. Chill dough for 45 minutes.
Roll into 1" balls and place on greased cookie sheet; bake at 350 degrees for 10
minutes. Immediately when removing from oven, place ½ Andes' mint on center of
each cookie. When chocolate melts; frost to spread more evenly on each cookie. Cool
until mint sets.

Homemade Oreos

1 pkg. Devils Food Cake Mix   2 eggs
¾ C shortening

Mix together cake mix, eggs and shortening. Roll into 1 inch balls; put on an ungreased
cookie sheet. Flatten slightly with the bottom of a glass. Bake at 375 for 8 minutes.
Cool and put 2 cookies together with filling.

Filling:
8 oz softened cream cheese   ¼ C butter
3 C powdered sugar   2 t vanilla

Mix softened cream cheese, butter and vanilla. Gradually add powdered sugar, beating
well.

Fresh Orange Cookies

1 ½ C sugar
1 C butter
2 eggs
4 C flour
1 t baking soda

1 t baking powder
½ t salt
⅔ C orange juice
3 T orange peel
1 C sour cream

Preheat oven to 375 degrees. Beat sugar and butter until light and fluffy. Add sour cream. Blend well. Stir in flour, baking powder, baking soda, salt, orange juice and orange peel. Mix well. Drop by rounded spoonfuls on ungreased cookie sheet. Bake 8 – 11 minutes, until edges are light brown. Remove immediately. Frost while still warm.

Frosting:
⅓ C butter
3 C powdered sugar

1 T orange peel
4-5 T orange juice

We would often come home from school and find these cookies waiting in the freezer. It was so easy to get them out, slice off as many cookies as we wanted, and bake them. Making homemade treats does not have to take up all your time. When you have a little extra time, make something great and stick it in the freezer. When you need a quick treat or meal, it is waiting for you. We have found that other people need things just when you are your busiest! We are not always prepared with something in the freezer, but it is nice when we are.

Grandma's Icebox Cookies

We don't remember these cookies, but my mom does. They come from her grandma Gulley and our Grandma McGee.

½ lb butter
1 C shortening
1 C brown sugar, packed
1 C sugar
3 eggs

5 C flour
1 T baking soda
1 C flaked coconut
1 t vanilla
pinch salt

Mix well, roll into waxed paper, and leave in refrigerator. Slice what you need and place on cookie sheets. Bake at 400 degrees for 10 minutes. These wrapped cookies also freeze well.

❧ ❧

We can't even tell you how many hundreds of dozens of these cookies we have made. Sugar cookies are a little more work, but they are worth it. Kerri may win the prize for the most sugar cookies ever made! She used to make dozens of them for my mom's students each year. A friend, Julie Smith, is known for her ghost cookies. She makes sugar cookies, drizzles some white glaze on them, then uses mini-chocolate chips for eyes and a mouth. They are great and an easy way to decorate these great cookies. Let your imagination run wild. Give some kids a bowl of frosting and a spoon and let them come up with the designs. Some things are worth the time and mess – these cookies may be one of those things. We're not saying that is what we would do – kids, bowls of frosting, clean-up for a week! – but it sounds like a fun idea. We are still trying to convince our mom to have "grandma cookie day" with all her grandchildren. That is never going to happen!

The Biggs Girl's Famous Sugar Cookies
this is our favorite sugar cookie recipe. Its original name was Mary's Sugar Cookies, but we have changed it over time and everyone has tried to claim it as their own. Martie tried to pass them off as "Martie's Sugar Cookies."

1 ½ C powdered sugar	½ t almond extract
1 C butter	2 ½ C flour
1 egg	1 t baking soda
1 t vanilla	1 t cream of tartar

Cream sugar and butter. Mix in egg and flavorings. Blend dry ingredients and stir in. Refrigerate for 30 minutes. Roll out on floured surface. Cut into shapes. Bake at 325 degrees for 7 – 8 minutes. Cool and frost.

Valentine's Day Frosting
½ C red hot cinnamon candies	½ C water
16 large marshmallows	2 C powdered sugar

Simmer rod hots and water until candies are melted. Remove from heat. Add marshmallows, stir until melted and add the sugar. Stir until smooth. Frost cooled sugar cookies with warm icing. This makes a beautiful, shiny, fun frosting.

❦

The famous little cinnamon candies are getting more and more difficult to find. We start looking for them to show up in bigger bags at the beginning of February. All the joys of certain holidays are disappearing – which is another reason you should make your own! We have found the cinnamon candies available for ordering on several internet sites. You can also use the bigger cinnamon flavored hard candies. The red color and intense cinnamon flavor is the most important. It is important to note that you can't stack these cookies if you have frosted them with the Valentine's Frosting. Take our word – you will have one giant, albeit great tasting, cookie clump!

Half – Hearted Cookies

¾ C sugar	1 egg
1 C butter	1 t peppermint extract
1 – 3oz pkg cream cheese	3 C flour

In large mixer, combine sugar, butter, cream cheese, egg, and peppermint. Beat at medium speed scraping bowl often, until light and fluffy, 3 – 4 minutes. Add flour and mix well. Divide dough in half, wrap in waxed paper, and chill for 2 hours.

Glaze:
1 C semi-sweet chocolate chips   ¼ C butter

Heat oven to 375 degrees. Roll out dough on lightly floured surface to ¼" thick. Cut into heart shaped cookies, place 1" apart on cookie sheets and bake for 7 – 8 minutes. Cool completely.

In small saucepan melt chocolate and butter over low heat. Dip half of each cooled cookie into glaze, place on waxed paper until glaze is firm. Makes about 3 dozen cookies.

Cherry Chocolate Kisses

1 C powdered sugar	2 ¼ C flour
1 C butter	½ t salt
2 t maraschino cherry juice	½ C maraschino cherries, chopped and drained
½ t almond extract	48 chocolate candy kisses unwrapped
few drops of red food coloring	

Heat oven to 350 degrees. In a large bowl, combine powdered sugar, butter, cherry juice, almond, and food coloring; mix well. Mix in flour and salt; stir in cherries. Shape dough into 1" balls. Place 2" apart on baking sheets. Bake for 8 – 10 minutes. Remove from oven and place one candy kiss in the center of each cookie. Cool.

Fortune Cookies

These are really fun to make because you can make your own "love notes" or fortunes to place inside the cookies. They make a great gift too!

1 egg	dash salt
½ C sugar	⅓ C milk
¼ C margarine melted	red food coloring (optional)
36 messages on strips of paper	

Beat egg slightly in medium bowl. Add sugar, margarine, almond, and food coloring. Mix in flour and salt. Add milk and mix until smooth and well blended. Spread one T of batter into 3" circle on hot surface of non-stick frying pan or electric skillet. Cook about 1 minute then turn and cook 1 minute more. Remove from skillet, place fortune in the center and fold in half. Place over rim of a glass and fold in half with points down to shape cookie. You will need to work quickly while cookie is warm. Let cool to harden.

❧ ❧

When Valayne's kids were very little, a good friend and neighbor started hosting Cookie Day every Friday after school. This neighbor made some really awesome cookies. The entire neighborhood would flock to her house after school on Fridays and fill themselves with warm and delicious cookies. They couldn't wait to see what kind of cookies waited for them after a long hard day of elementary school. Valayne continued Cookie Day in several places they lived, but her friend Karyn will always be the Friday Cookie Day neighbor. Few kids can resist free cookies and it is a great way to meet new friends in your neighborhoods. This recipe is one of our favorites from a good friend. Thanks Karyn. (We still want your cinnamon roll recipe!)

Crispie Chocolate Chip Cookies

1 C margarine	1 C oil
1 C brown sugar	1 C sugar
1 egg	2 t vanilla
1 t coconut flavoring	3 ½ C flour
1 t salt	1 t baking soda
1 C quick cooking oats	1 C coconut flakes
1 C crisp rice cereal	12 oz chocolate chips – white, milk, or semi-sweet
1 t cream of tartar	

Cream margarine, oil, and sugars. Add egg and flavorings. Stir in flour, salt, and soda. Mix well. Add other ingredients. Drop by teaspoonfuls on lightly greased cookie sheets. Bake at 350 degrees for 12 minutes.

Butterfinger Cookies

½ C butter, softened
2/3 C packed brown sugar
1 ¼ C chunky peanut butter
1 C flour
¼ t salt

¾ C sugar
1 egg
1 ½ t vanilla extract
½ t baking soda
5 Butterfinger candy bars (2.1 ounces each),
    coarsely chopped

In a mixing bowl, cream butter and sugars together. Add egg; beat well. Blend in peanut butter and vanilla. Combine flour, baking soda and salt; add to creamed mixture and mix well. Stir in candy bars. Shape into 1 ½ inch balls; place on greased baking sheets. Bake at 350 deegrees for 10-12 minutes or until golden brown. Makes about 4 dozen.

Dreamsicle Cookies –

These cookies really do taste just like the orange and ice cream bars!

½ C orange instant breakfast powder
1 cube butter softened
1 t vanilla
1 ¾ C flour
½ t baking soda

¾ C sugar
1 egg
1 ½ C vanilla chips
½ t baking powder

Cream butter, sugar, and drink mix. Add egg and vanilla. Mix in dry ingredients until well blended. Shape into 1" balls and bake at 375 for 12 – 14 minutes. Makes 2 ½ dozen cookies. These cookies can be changed to suit your own tastes and mood. You can vary the flavor of drink mix and chips. You can add nuts or other candies. Raspberry drink mix combines well with semi-sweet chocolate chips. Sweetened chocolate or espresso mix combines great with toffee chips. Let your imagination run wild!

We have given as many cookies away as we have made, maybe more. Cookies do take some time to bake. You can eliminate that time in a couple of ways if you are in a time crunch – and who isn't most of the time?! You can mix up a batch of cookies and place all the dough in a 13 X 9 pan or sheet pan – depending on the amount of dough you have. Bake them and cut them into bars. You can also layer the dry ingredients in a clear container, attach the recipe, and let the recipient make the cookies up by adding the wet ingredients when they have time. This works well for all kinds of recipes from cakes to soups.

Pumpkin Cookies

½ C shortening

1 egg

½ C nuts

1 t vanilla

1 t nutmeg

1 t ground cinnamon

½ t salt

1 ½ C sugar

1 C canned pumpkin

1 C raisins (optional)

2 ½ C flour

1 t baking powder

1 t baking soda

chocolate chips

Cream shortening and sugar; add flavoring and egg. Mix dry ingredients together and add to creamed mixture. Stir in nuts and chips. Bake at 375 for 12 minutes.

We had some neighbors growing up in the country – back when Gilbert was way out in the country. They had cows, horses, four boys, and one daughter. We were good friends and did almost everything together. We built a tree house together and splept many summer nights in it. Her name is Deanna and she was always a hard worker. It was not easy for her growing up with all those brothers. We loved going to their house. It was so different from ours, that was filled with all girls. We spent lot of time in their family kitchen. Deanna's brothers would bring in the milk from the cow. She would take the bucket with manure bits and dirt chunks floating on top, pour it through a cheesecloth while another person held the corners of the cloth to keep it from falling into the gallon jar. This process would strain the dead flies and other bits of things from the milk. Waxed paper and lid were then placed on top, and the ready to drink milk was thrown in the fridge. We never drank milk much after that! Most of us still cringe at the sight of it. We would often make these cookies together in Deanna's kitchen, after all her chores were done. We would eat some of them and try to keep her brothers from eating all of them as soon as they came out of the oven. It was tough, but we always managed to have a few left to share with a neighbor.

Cowboy Cookies

1 C shortening	½ t salt
1 C sugar	1 t baking soda
1 C brown sugar packed	1 t baking powder
2 eggs	2 C flour
1 t vanilla	2 C quick cooking oats
Chocolate chips	

Cream shorting and sugars; add eggs and flavoring. Mix dry ingredients and add to creamed mixture. Stir in nuts and chips. Drop by spoonfuls onto cookie sheets. Bake at 350 degrees for 12 minutes.

Orange-Spiced Oatmeal Raisin Cookies Dipped in White Chocolate

¾ C raisins	3 T orange juice
½ C butter, softened	¾ C sugar
1 large egg	2 t grated orange peel
1 C flour	1 t baking soda
1 ½ C quick oats	8 oz white chocolate chips
1 t vegetable oil or shortening	

Combine orange juice and raisins and let stand several hours or overnight. Beat butter and sugar until fluffy; add egg, vanilla, and orange peel. Combine dry ingredients and mix into creamed mixture. Stir in soaked raisins and oats. Drop by spoonfuls onto cookie sheet and flatten slightly. Bake at 350 degrees for 10-12 minutes. In a small bowl, microwave chocolate and oil 3-4 minutes on low power. Stir until smooth. Dip cooled cookies into chocolate and place on waxed paper until set. Makes about 3 dozen.

Almond Bonbons
Cookies

3 C flour	1 C butter (softened)
2/3 C powdered sugar	6 T milk
1 tsp vanilla	1 pkg almond paste (7 or 8oz size)

Heat oven to 375 degrees. In Large bowl, beat flour, butter sugar, milk and the vanilla with electric mixer on medium. Cut almond paste into ½ inch slices; cut each slice into 8 pieces. Shape 1 inch ball of dough around each piece of almond paste. Gently roll to form ball. On ungreased cookie sheet, place balls about 1 inch apart. Bake 10 – 12 minutes or until set and bottoms are golden brown. Remove from cookie sheet and cool completely about 30 minutes.

Frosting

2 C powdered sugar	1 t almond extract
8 to 10 t milk	

Decoration – edible glitter, white candy sprinkles or coarse sugar

In small bowl, mix all frosting ingredients with spoon until smooth. Dip tips of cookies into frosting. Sprinkle with edible glitter.

Oatmeal Apple Butter Cookies

¾ C butter flavored shortening	1 C brown sugar
½ C sugar	1 egg
¼ C water	1 t vanilla
1 C flour	1 t salt
½ t baking soda	3 C quick oats
Apple Butter or jam of your choice	

Cream shortening, sugars, vanilla, egg, water, and baking soda. Stir in flour and oats. Scoop batter into rounded balls onto a greased cookie sheet. Make an indentation in the scooped batter with the back of the cookie scoop. Pour a little spoon full of apple butter or jam into the indentation. Bake at 350 degrees for 12 to 15 minutes.

Biscotti
Mix:

2 eggs   ¾ C sugar
¾ C oil

Add:

2 T orange extract   ½ C dried cranberries

Mix together:

2 ½ C flour   2 t baking powder
Add flour mixture to other ingredients and combine well.

Divide dough into to loaves a foot long by about 5 inches wide. Place on cookie sheet and bake at 375 degrees for about 20 minutes. Slice each loaf into one inch pieces.

Cookie Pizza

½ C margarine, softened	1 egg
½ C Peanut butter	1 t vanilla
½ C sugar	1 ½ C flour
½ C brown sugar	2 C miniature marshmallows
1 C chocolate chips	1 C chopped nuts

Cream margarine, peanut butter, and sugars. Beat in egg and vanilla. Stir in flour until blended. Spread dough onto greased, 12" pizza pan. Bake at 375 degrees for 12 minutes. Sprinkle with chocolate chips, marshmallows, and nuts. Bake 5-6 minutes longer or until lightly browned.

New Recipes

~ *Popcorn and Cereal* ~

❧❧

I'm not sure how many batches of this yummy caramel corn my mom made, but she used to buy the 50-gallon bag of pre-popped corn on a regular basis! She taught school and used to make huge batches for her students and co-workers. This recipe makes a great gift, snack, and easy treat to share with a group. It is much easier to find a store that sells already popped corn in a bag. You may also try your favorite movie theater. Many theaters will sell their popped corn even if you don't watch a movie there.

Caramel Popcorn

20 C popped corn   2 cubes margarine
½ C light corn syrup   2 C brown sugar

Boil over medium heat for 6 minutes. Take off heat and add:
¼ t cream of tartar   ½ t salt
1 t baking soda

Pour over popped corn in a large mixing bowl. Mix well to coat all kernels. Pour out onto greased baking sheet. Bake at 200 degrees for 1 hour. Stir every 20 minutes.

Chocolate Popcorn

Pop 2 regular size bags of microwave popcorn. Pick out the un-popped kernels and put the popped corn into a large bowl.

In a sauce pan cook just until melted:
¾ cups butter   ¾ cups brown sugar
2 ½ cups mini marshmallows

Pour over popcorn and stir to coat. Then dump coated popcorn onto a large cookie sheet, and spread it out.

Melt in microwave in separate containers:
4 oz chocolate chips (milk or dark, which ever you prefer.)
4 oz white chocolate chips

Drizzle over popcorn, when the chocolate is set it is ready to eat, if you can wait that long. A few minutes in the freezer or fridge speeds the process, but don't forget it in the freezer for too long.

❧❦

We have had people beg us for this recipe. One friend of Valayne's called her from out of town to get this recipe to share with her family when she was traveling to visit them. It is a quick easy treat that is amazingly good! It is not unusual for us to get emergency recipe phone calls. We call each other for recipes or new ideas when we are in the baking mood. Our kids call us from all over the country to get recipes to make for friends or their dates.

White Chocolate Caramel Corn

6 boxes deluxe caramel corn with nuts
2 large hunks almond bark or 1 bag white chocolate chips

Melt white chocolate and pour over caramel corn in large mixing bowl. Spread out on cookie sheet and let cool until chocolate is set.

Sticky Gooey Caramel Corn

1 1/3 C sugar	½ C cashews
1 C butter	½ C almonds
1 t Vanilla	Any nuts you like
½ C light corn syrup	8 – 10 C popcorn

Bring sugar, butter, vanilla, and syrup to a boil; boil until it turns a light caramel color (about 5 minutes.) In large bowl stir together popcorn & nuts. Pour sugar mixture over popcorn and stir until thoroughly coated. Let cool if you can before eating.

❧❦

Our grandma McGee (Gee) used to make treats for several holidays during the year. Puffed rice balls were her Halloween treat. She always had a bag full to send home with my mom for all of us. Even after we were all married, she made puffed rice balls for each family, carefully making sure we all had the same amount. They might be an acquired taste for some, but we all love them. They are not the same without my grandma, but they are a loved family tradition and fond memory about someone we all loved.

Grandma's Puffed Rice Balls

3 C sugar	1 C water
1 C light corn syrup	dash salt
softened butter	

Boil to soft ball stage and pour over several cups of puffed rice cereal. Let cool slightly, enough to handle with hands. Butter hands and form into balls. Let cool completely. Cover each ball with waxed paper and enjoy on Halloween!

Fudge Crispies

12 oz milk chocolate chips	½ C margarine
½ C light corn syrup	2 t vanilla
1 C sifted powdered sugar	4 C rice cereal

Melt chocolate, margarine, and corn syrup over low heat. Mix in remaining ingredients. Press into buttered funnel to shape like "kisses" or into buttered 13 X 9 pan.

Gooey Cereal Mix

We got this recipe from LaDawn Goodman, and it has also become a family favorite. It makes a great teacher gift, bagged and bowed.

Stir together in a large bowl.

8 C rice cereal squares   8 C corn cereal squares

1 ½ C nuts

1 C coconut (We like the wide toasted ribbons, it looks lovely, but the shredded works too.)

In a saucepan over medium high heat; combine:

1 ½ C sugar   1 ½ C light corn syrup

1 C butter

Boil for 2 ½ minutes. Then add 1 tsp vanilla. Stir and pour over mixture in large bowl. Stir until coated; pour and spread onto a large cookie sheet and let sit until cool.

~ *Gelatins* ~

꧁꧂

There is a sort of "pecking order" in our family when it comes to food. When we get together we always have food, and everyone brings something to share. The host usually organizes the event and the menu. Everyone is assigned a dish of some kind. As people make the transition from child to adult, they are given an assignment and that first assignment is usually a salad or gelatin. You have to prove yourself before you are given a more weighty assignment. We thought Kerri would never move up to a "real" food assignment. She had some issues with lemon-lime gelatin. (In her defense, it is a tricky recipe and takes some time and advanced planning.) Jana is the exception to the gelatin rule. She is famous for her pretzel gelatin and we often ask her to bring that because it is so good and she is best at making it.

We have added a "gelatin course" to almost every meal we have. With such picky eaters, it is a great way to sneak in a fruit (and sometimes a vegetable) without kids even knowing it! A meal just isn't a meal without some kind of gelatin or fruit salad.

Jeanette's Gelatin

1 large pkg. Red gelatin (whatever flavor you like)

First layer – make gelatin according to directions on box. Pour into a 9X13 pan and let set in the refrigerator.

½ pint whipping cream	1 C sugar
1 pkg. Knox gelatin	½ C hot water
2 C sour cream	1 t vanilla

Second Layer – over medium heat in a saucepan; mix whipping cream and sugar. Mix 1 pkg of Knox gelatin in the ½ c. hot water and then add it to the mixture in the saucepan. Add sour cream and vanilla; mix until smooth. Let cool and then pour carefully over first layer (gelatin), let set in the refrigerator.

1 sm pkg red gelatin (any flavor- does not have to be the same as the first layer.)
1 C hot water

1pkg. Frozen fruit (raspberries, strawberries or blue berries or a combination.)

Third Layer – Mix 1 c. hot water & red gelatin until gelatin is dissolved. Add fruit; stir; pour on top of second layer. Let set in the refrigerator.

LeElla's Gelatin

1 large box red gelatin (any flavor)

Prepare as directed on box; pour into 9x13 pan. Refrigerate until set, and then start the second layer.

1 small box red gelatin (any flavor)	1 C boiling water
1 – 8 oz pkg cream cheese	1 C powdered sugar
1 small container of frozen whipped topping (thawed)	

Stir small box gelatin and boiling water until gelatin is dissolved; set aside to cool. Combine cream cheese and powdered sugar. Fold in whipped topping. Mix in cooled gelatin and pour over first layer. Let set in refrigerator.

Cherry Rice Gelatin
Eric's favorite

1 large box cherry gelatin   2 C boiling water
10 ice cubes   ½ C sugar
1 large can crushed pineapple   2 ½ C cooked minute rice
40 maraschino cherries (chopped)   2 pts. Frozen whipped topping (thawed)
1 c. chopped nuts (walnuts)

Mix together Gelatin and boiling water until dissolved; then add ice, sugar, pineapple, rice, and cherries. Refrigerate until it is medium firm. Stir in whipped topping and nuts. Refrigerate until ready to serve.

Pretzel Gelatin
Crust:
1 cube melted butter   ⅓ C sugar
2 C crushed pretzels (not pulverized, more like broken)

Mix well and spread in the bottom of a 13x9 pan. Bake at 400 for 8 min. Cool completely before adding next layer.

Middle Layer:
1 – 8 oz cream cheese   1 C sugar
8 oz frozen whipped topping (thawed)

Mix well until smooth and creamy. Spread evenly over cooled crust. It is very important that this is spread to the edges and it makes a seal completely around the pan.

Final Layer:
2 C boiling water   2 small pkgs. Strawberry Gelatin
2 – 10 oz pkg. frozen strawberries

Dissolve gelatins in boiling water, add strawberries. Set in refrigerator until partially set, then pour over middle layer. Refrigerate until set and ready to serve.

Rainbow Gelatin

1 small box green gelitin	1 small box yellow Gelatin
1 small box orange Gelatin	1 small box red Gelatin
1 small box purple Gelatin (grape)	2 ½ C sour cream

In five separate bowls, mix one box of Gelatin with 1 C boiling water. Divide each bowl in half (about 2/3 C) into another five bowls. To each half add ½ C sour cream. To the other halves add 2 T cold water. You will now have 5 bowls of Gelatin without sour cream and 5 bowls with sour cream.

Pour red gelatin without sour cream into the bottom of 13 X 9 pan and chill until set. Pour red gelatin with sour cream over red set gelatin and chill until set. Continue with oranges, then yellows, then greens, and finally purples. OK, this gelatin takes some time to make, but it turns out really beautiful!

&

As mentioned above, there is kind of a pecking order when it comes to bringing food to a family get-together. If you are a new cook/adult being asked to bring something, you are assigned a salad or gelatin dish. It is difficult to mess up a salad or gelitin – although my sisters have messed up gelatin. If you prove yourself in the salad area, next time you get a more complicated assignment until you can bring what you want. If you are told to bring what you want or something that goes with the main dish, it is the nod that you are accomplished enough to decide what to bring and that you can make just about anything. Lemon – Lime Gelatin is one of our basic gelatin assignments. Kerri has mastered this and moved on now! But, only recently!

Chris Nichols' Lemon – Lime Gelatin

1 small box Lime Gelatin	1C boiling water

1 – 8oz frozen whipped topping (thawed)
1 small box Cook and Serve (not instant) Lemon Pudding

Mix Lime Gelatin with 1 cup boiling water. Make Lemon pudding according to package directions. Carefully stir the hot gelatin and the hot pudding together; pour them into a 9x13 pan and refrigerate until set. Before serving spread whipped topping over the top.

New Recipes

~ *Candies and Confections* ~

❧❧

Food is always about so much more than just eating. We can make food into a gift, into an object lesson (as with the fudge recipe below), into a party, into a reason to get together, into a contest, a pecking order, a source of comfort, an apology, and as an essential part of any trip! Food is always more than just something to eat in our family, and probably yours too. Some candy recipes are traditions for specific holidays or events. It just wouldn't be Christmas without caramels. Grandma McGee used to make caramels for every family. The caramels were wrapped in waxed paper and bagged for each family. Start a family tradition of your own with one or more of these great recipes.

Handmade Fudge
Great for a Demo speech or an object lesson

1 lb powdered sugar	3 oz. Cream cheese
1 cube of butter	½ C of Cocoa
1 t vanilla	

Combine the above ingredients in a gallon size zip bag. Pass around in a group, letting each one squeeze the bag with the intent of having the ingredient mix together.

Each ingredient is unique and different and alone doesn't necessarily have the most appetizing taste. But when it's mixed together, worked through, and completely blended, you have something wonderfully sweet. Alone, a job, task or an activity may seem difficult and dull. But when done all together, the task at hand seems to go by so much quicker, with much more ease, and has a much sweeter result.

81

Chocolate Butter Fudge

3 C sugar
½ C light corn syrup
1 envelope unflavored gelatin
1 C milk

1 ¼ C margarine
2 t vanilla
1 C chopped nuts
3 squares unsweetened chocolate

Mix sugar and gelatin in saucepan. Add milk, syrup, chocolate, and margarine; cook over medium heat stirring frequently until candy reaches 238 degrees or soft ball stage. Remove from heat and pour into mixing bowl; add vanilla. Cool 15 minutes. Beat until candy thickens, stir in nuts, and spread on buttered baking pan. Cut into 1" squares.

Grandma's Fudge

1 cube butter
1 can evaporated milk (2/3 c)
1 jar marshmallow cream

2 C sugar
1 pkg chocolate chips
chopped nuts (optional)

Boil together sugar, butter, and milk for 5 minutes on low stirring frequently. Remove from heat and stir in chocolate, marshmallow cream, and nuts. Pour into buttered dish to cool. Cut into 1" squares.

❧❧

Ella Mae was a friend of grandma McGee's. Grandma and grandpa used to play cards with Ella Mae and her husband. We have fond memories of going to Ella Mae's house, watching the adults play cards, and connecting her to grandma's "Fish Bait Fudge." Ella Mae didn't look like she ever ate fudge. She was very tall and skinny. "Fish Bait Fudge" comes from the fact that we use Velveta for fish bait when fishing with our dad. We had a bit of a hard time as kids knowing this fudge was made with "fish bait." It tastes really good and creamy though, so we got over it.

Ella Mae's Fudge

1 lb Velveta cheese
4 lbs powdered sugar
2 t vanilla

1 lb margarine
1 C cocoa powder
2 C nuts

Melt cheese and margarine on low heat. Add 1 lb of the sugar and the cocoa powder over heat. Blend until smooth. Add remaining sugar while stirring over heat. Bring to boil, remove from heat, and add vanilla and nuts. Pour into 13 X 9 pan and let cool. Cut into 1 " squares.

Chocolate Fudge

2 ¾ C sugar   4 oz unsweetened chocolate
3 T butter   1 C half and half
1 T corn syrup   1 T vanilla
1 C chopped nuts

Grease an 8 X 8 pan with butter. In a heavy saucepan on medium heat, combine sugar, chocolate, 1 ½ T of the butter, milk and corn syrup. After chocolate is melted, turn up heat and bring to a boil. Reduce heat to medium and cook for 3 minutes with a lid on. Remove cover and cook until 234 degrees. Remove from heat and add remaining butter. Let cool then add vanilla and nuts. Stir mixture until it becomes dull in hue – no longer shiny. Pour into prepared pan. Cut into 1" squares.

Lynne's Grandma Mally's Pulled Mints

2 C sugar   1 C hot water
2 oz butter

Cook to 260 degrees without stirring. Pour out onto marble slab or other heatproof surface to cool. Add flavoring and color when edges are cool.

Stretch and pull like salt-water taffy until it begins to feel dried out. Roll into strips and cut into ½" pieces. Roll in mixture of 1 part powdered sugar and one part cornstarch. Let cool completely. Store in airtight container.

Candied Nuts

1 pound shelled nuts   1 egg white
1 T water   1 C sugar
1 t salt   1 t cinnamon

Beat egg white and water until frothy. Pour over nuts. Combine sugar and spices and pour over coated nuts. Spread on large cookie sheet and bake at 275 for 45 minutes. Stir every 15 minutes. Cool.

ॐ◌ॐ

Our grandma McGee (Gee) used to make treats for several holidays during the year. This caramel recipe and peanut brittle recipe are ones she used to make at Christmas time. She and my grandpa lived in a tiny four-room house for most of their adult lives. We had Christmas and Thanksgiving dinners there until grandma became too ill to host. We used to eat outside on the carport. Grandma's tiny kitchen was full of cooks (moms) while kids and dads watched football games or shot baskets in the hoop outside in the back yard. Grandma made batches of caramels and wrapped the squares in waxed paper for even distribution to families.

Grandma's Caramels

2 C sugar   1 ¾ C light corn syrup
2 C cream (divided)   ¼ cube margarine
Dash salt

Boil together all ingredients except one cup of the cream. Boil 30 minutes stirring occasionally, add 2nd cup of cream; boil and stir to firm ball. Add chopped nuts and pour into buttered pan. Cool and cut into 1-inch squares. Wrap in waxed paper.

Lynne's Caramels

1 C butter or margarine   1 – 16 oz pkg br. Sugar (2 ½ C)
dash salt   1 C light corn syrup
1 – 14 oz can sweetened condensed milk
1 t vanilla

Butter a 9 x 9 x 2" pan. Melt butter in heavy saucepan, add sugar, salt and stir until melted. Stir in corn syrup. Gradually add milk. Cook over medium heat to 245 degrees (firm ball) about 12 – 15 minutes. Remove, add vanilla, cut into squares and wrap in waxed paper.

*Marti thinks **her** caramel recipe is the best. She doesn't like to be outdone and won't admit it even if she is. We do think her's are pretty good caramels. You may not always have sweetened condensed milk on hand (like our sister Kerri who buys it by the case and cracks open a can when she wants a sweet treat and eats it right out of the can) so this is a good alternative.*

Caramels

2 C sugar
2 C light corn syrup
Nuts (optional)

1 cube butter
2 C cream

Cook sugar and corn syrup to a soft ball stage. Add butter and stir until melted. Add cream and stir often over medium heat until it is at the firm ball stage. Add nuts, stir and pour into a buttered 9x13 pan. Cut into ½ " x 1" rectangles when cool and wrap in waxed paper.

Our mom used to make this special candy at Christmas time. It is very rich. It was a very special treat and we never made it any other time of the year. We didn't have candy very much and pies were my mom's thing, so this home made candy was a rare treat.

Cream Candy

1 C cream
2 T light corn syrup

1 C sugar

Cook over medium heat stirring occasionally to soft ball stage. Add a pinch of salt and pour onto buttered cookie sheet. Add chopped nuts and stir until candy becomes thick and grainy. Prepare waxed paper covered with coconut flakes. Spoon thickened candy onto coconut-covered waxed paper and roll into 1" log. Cool completely and slice into ½" slices.

Grandma's Peanut Brittle
Another Christmas tradition

2 C sugar
1 big bag raw peanuts

1 C light corn syrup

Cook sugar and corn syrup until light tan, add nuts, and then add 2 heaping t baking soda. Spread on two cookies sheets and let cool.

New Recipes

~ *Frozen Treats* ~

❦

Valayne was teaching her 7th grade English class one day about personal narratives and how one goes about writing one. She gave an example that involved a family memory about homemade ice cream. Almost immediately, in every one of her classes, when she would get to the part about the ice cream, hands shot up like crazy. Not one of her students had the slightest idea you could actually make ice cream. She had a difficult time convincing them it was possible. She promised that before the year was over they would make ice cream in class and enjoy it together. We can't imagine a life with never having experienced homemade ice cream. It is not that difficult to make. It does require some time and an investment in an ice cream maker. I know there are all kinds on the market and many of the more popular ones are those that require you to freeze the bowl of the machine. I like the more traditional method and machine that require ice and rock salt. We don't recommend the hand cranking, but it does keep small children busy! There are just some things everyone should experience, and homemade ice cream is one of those things. Make some and share.

Sistersfamilyrecipes@gmail.com

Mom's Vanilla Ice Cream

6 eggs
2 C sugar
1 pint heavy cream
Whole milk

1 qt half and half
1 can sweetened condensed milk
3 T vanilla (really great with vanilla beans)

Beat eggs very well; add sugar, cream, half and half, and condensed milk. Pour into canister of 6-quart ice cream freezer. Fill to full line with whole milk. Freeze according to directions.

Variations include but are not limited to:
Almond Joy ice cream – Add 1 c. coconut, 1 c. chopped and toasted almonds, 1 package mini chocolate chips and 2 tsp. Almond extract and 1 tsp. coconut flavoring.
Toffee bar or snickers or any of your favorite candy bars or a combination of them ice cream – smash 12 candy bars and add them.
Chocolate mint ice cream – 8 drops green food coloring, 1 T. mint flavoring, and 1 package of mini chocolate chips.
Pistachio almond ice cream – 8 drops green food coloring, 1 T. almond flavoring, 1 cup shelled pistachios.

❧❧

This basic ice cream recipe can be modified into just about any flavor you can think of. Add your favorite fruits, candy, flavorings (root beer is one of our favorites), or powders (like malt powder with malted milk balls – one of my favorites). We had peach trees growing up and our dad loved fresh peach ice cream. Another family favorite was crushed toffee candy bars.

Charlotte's Blackberry Ice Cream

2 T lemon juice
½ C light corn syrup
2 ⅔ C sugar
1 ½ quarts whipping cream

1 ½ pounds frozen blackberries (can use fresh)
8 egg yolks
2 C milk

Thaw berries and blend with lemon juice; blend in corn syrup. Beat egg yolks with sugar until light and fluffy. Combine with blackberry mixture and pour into canister of 6-quart freezer. Add milk and cream. Freeze according to directions. Makes 6 quarts.

Rocky Road Ice Cream

3-4 eggs	1 small package chocolate instant pudding
1 C sugar	1 can sweetened condensed milk
1 quart ½ & ½	3 ½ pints whipping cream
1 C Hershey's chocolate Syrup	1 ⅔ C mini marshmallows
1 T vanilla	1 C chopped and toasted almonds

Mix first seven ingredients together until well blended especially the eggs. Stir in remaining ingredients and pour into a 1 ½ qt. Ice Cream freezer and freeze.

Tropical Ice Cream Dessert

½ gallon pineapple sherbet   Any size container frozen whipped topping
Mothers macaroon cookies, crumbled
½ - 1 C sliced or slivered almonds

Thaw ice cream slightly and add all other ingredients. Re-freeze and serve.

Chocolate Mint Ice Cream Pie

Process whole package of Chocolate Teddy grahams and mix with ¼ c. melted butter. Put half of mix at bottom of 13x9 pan, drizzle with Mrs. Richardson Hot Fudge Topping. Add 1.5 qt. softened Chocolate Mint ice cream. Sprinkle other half of cookie mixture over the ice cream. Re-freeze.

Praline Ice Cream Pie

1 ½ C flour	1 ½ C brown sugar
¾ C cold butter	1 ½ C chopped pecans

Mix in food processor. Spread on cookie sheet and bake 10-15 min. at 350. Let cool. Crumble and layer half of mix in bottom of 13x9" pan. Drizzle half a jar of caramel topping over crust. Spread over crust, 1.5 qt. of softened butter pecan ice cream. Spread on rest of crumbly mix and other half of caramel topping. Cover and re-freeze.

Balsamic Berry Sauce for Ice Cream

10-oz bag frozen mixed berries   3 T balsamic vinegar
1 t cornstarch

Combine berries and balsamic vinegar in saucepan over medium heat. Bring to a simmer and cook, stirring often, 5 minutes or until the berries become liquid. In a small bowl, combine the cornstarch with 2 T. cold water. Add this mixture to the berries and cook, stirring constantly, until the sauce thickens. Let cool for several minutes, then drizzle over ice cream.

We are not sure where this recipe originated, but back in the day it was a family staple dessert. It is easy to make, and can be modified to please your audience or your own taste. The strawberries and gelatin can be replaced with chocolate pudding or pistachio pudding. Be creative and try something new. It would be difficult for this recipe not to taste good. It has one of our favorite ingredients – cream cheese! Everything tastes better with cream cheese and butter!

Danish Dessert

Crust:
2/3 C powdered sugar   2 C flour
1 C butter (softened)   1 C chopped nuts

Mix, press in 9x13 pan. Bake at 375 for 15 minutes. Cool completely before adding the filling layer.

Filling:
1 C powdered sugar   1 – 8oz cream cheese
1 Small frozen whipped topping (thawed)

Beat powdered sugar and cream cheese until smooth; fold in cool whip. Spread over crust.

Topping:
1 C sugar   1 small box strawberry Gelatin
1 T cornstarch   1 C boiling water
1 box frozen strawberries

Cook first four ingredients until clear and foam disappears. Add strawberries stir until melted. Pour over filling; refrigerate until topping is set.

Mock-Fried Ice Cream

¾ C brown sugar
⅓ C coconut
½ C melted butter

2 ½ C crisp rice cereal
1 C chopped nuts (Toasted slivered Almonds)
½ gallon softened vanilla ice cream

Grease 9x13 pan. Mix all ingredients, except ice cream, and put in pan. Bake for 30 minutes at 300; stir with spatula every 10 minutes. Remove from oven and take out about 1/3 of mixture and set aside. Press remaining mixture in the bottom of the 9x13 pan. When cool spread ice cream over the crust and sprinkle with the reserved crumb mixture. Freeze; cut in squares and serve with topping.

Topping:
1 C sugar
1 ¾ C water
1 t vanilla

2 T cornstarch
1 large box Raspberry Gelatin
1 C Raspberries or strawberries

Cook first 3 ingredients until thick. Remove from heat and add Gelatin and vanilla. Stir until smooth. Cool a little then add berries. Serve over Fried Ice Cream.

Chocolate Peppermint Dessert

Crust:
1 ½ C crushed vanilla wafers
½ C melted butter

Combine and press in bottom of 9x13 pan. Bake at 350 degrees for 15 min.

Filling:
3 squares melted chocolate
¾ C butter (softened)

1 ½ C powdered sugar
3 eggs separated

Cream powdered sugar and butter; add melted chocolate. Beat in egg yolks. Beat 3gg whites until stiff, then fold into chocolate mixture. Spread over cooled crust.

Top layer:
2 C cream
1 C peppermint candy
4-6 drops red food coloring

¾ C powdered sugar
60 miniature marshmallows

Whip cream while adding the sugar. Crush candy. Cut miniature marshmallows in half. Fold candy and marshmallows and coloring into whipped cream. Spread over chocolate layer. Freeze until ready to serve.

Strawberry Mock Ice Cream

Crust:

¾ C packed brown sugar	2 C flour
1 C nuts	1 cube butter

Combine until crumbly. Place on cookie sheet. Bake 20 min. at 350. Cool and place ½ of mixture in 9x13 pan.

Filling:

1 package frozen strawberries	2 T lemon juice
1 C cream (whipped)	2 egg whites
2/3 C sugar	

Beat egg whites until stiff. Add sugar and berries and lemon juice. Beat until stiff again. Fold in whipped cream. Pour over crust. Sprinkle remaining crust on top. Freeze until ready to serve.

Frozen Raspberry Macadamia Dessert

Crust:

1 C crushed vanilla cookies	½ C finely chopped macadamia nuts
¼ C margarine melted	

Filling:

14 oz can sweetened condensed milk	3 T lemon juice
3 T orange juice	10 oz pkg frozen raspberries with syrup, thawed
1 C whipping cream, whipped	chocolate filigree hearts

Heat oven to 375. In small bowl, combine all crust ingredients; mix well. Press firmly into bottom of 8" spring form pan. Bake for 8 – 10 minutes. Cool.

In large bowl, combine milk and juices; beat until smooth. Add raspberries; beat at low speed until well blended. Fold in whipped cream. Pour over cooled crust. Freeze until firm – several hours or overnight. Let stand at room temperature about 15 minutes before serving. Garnish with chocolate hearts.

Chocolate filigree hearts:

1 oz semi sweet chocolate	1 t shortening

Melt and cool slightly. Place in small squeeze bottle or zip bag with one corner cut off. Draw a small 2" heart on white paper. Cut 12 3 X 3" squares out of waxed paper. Place each paper over heart pattern one at a time and pipe chocolate out following pattern. Fill in outline with swirls and lines, making sure all lines are connected to each other at some point. Let set in refrigerator for about 30 minutes. Decorate top of dessert with hearts.

Chocolate Cream Filled Cookie Raspberry Dessert

¼ C margarine   30 Chocolate cream filled cookies, crushed finely

Mix thoroughly and press into a 9X13 pan.

Soften 1 gallon of vanilla ice cream and spoon ½ of it into crust. Put one can of raspberry pie filling on top of ice cream, spoon remaining ice cream on top and sprinkle with a few crushed cookies. Freeze until set.

Wedding or Party Slush

1 sm. Gelatin any flavor you want ½ C lemon Juice
1 C sugar   ½ t Almond extract
3 C water   2 liters 7 up
1 large can pineapple juice

Dissolve Gelatin in 1 cup boiling water; add 1 c. sugar, 3 c. water, pineapple juice, lemon juice and ½ tsp extract. Pour in 1 gallon recloseable top freezer bag and freeze. Mash before serving and pour pop over it in a punch bowl.

New Recipes

~ *Miscellaneous* ~

✦

There are just a few great things that didn't fit into any of the categories we had listed above, but we couldn't leave them out. They are here in their own little group. The bread pudding recipes are some of our favorites. There is something so comforting about a warm dessert right out of the oven, not to mention the wonderful aromas during cooking. No need to wait for a special occasion to make something to warm those around you.

Caramel Sauce

½ C sugar   2 T light corn syrup

Cook over low heat until dissolved. Turn up heat to caramelize. Once liquid turns a light caramel color add 2/3 C heavy cream. Be careful as mixture will steam and solidify. Cook and stir over medium heat until dissolved.

Raspberry Pretzel Delight

Crust:
1 ½ C crushed pretzels   ¼ C sugar
½ C melted butter

Filling:
1 (21 oz.) can sweetened condensed milk
½ C water
1 (3.4 oz.) pkg. instant vanilla or white chocolate pudding mix
4 oz. (1 ¾ C) frozen whipped topping, thawed

Topping:
1 (21 oz.) can raspberry fruit pie filling

Heat oven to 350 degrees. In large bowl, combine all crust ingredients; mix well. Press into ungreased 13x9 pan. Bake at 350 degrees for 8 minutes; cool.

In same large bowl, combine condensed milk and water; blend well. Beat in pudding mix for 2 minutes. Refrigerate 5 minutes. Fold in whipped topping. Spread on cooled crust. Refrigerate until filling is firm, about 1 hour.

Spoon fruit topping over filling. Cover; refrigerate until serving time.

3 Layer Pumpkin Dessert

1st Layer:
2 c. graham cracker crumbs   1 cube butter, melted
1/3 c. sugar

Press into 13x9 pan and bake at 375 for 9 min.

2nd Layer:
8 oz cream Cheese   2 T milk
2 T sugar   1- 8 oz frozen whipped topping (thawed)

Spread on cooled crust.

3rd Layer:
1 ½ C milk   2 lg. boxes instant vanilla pudding
24 oz. can pumpkin   2 t cinnamon
¾ t ginger   ¼ t cloves

Spread over cream cheese layer.

Turtles with a Twist

1 bag small twist pretzels   2 bags round, chocolate covered, caramel candy
1 bag pecan halves

Place pretzels on foiled cookie sheet with a little space between each one. Top each pretzel with a candy. Bake at 350 degrees just enough to slightly soften. Remove from oven and top with a pecan half.

Nut Diamonds

1 C flour	½ C unsalted butter (cold)
½ C sugar	½ C brown sugar
2 T honey	¼ C cream
2 C mixed nuts	

Preheat oven to 350 degrees. Grease 9" square pan; line with foil; grease foil. In food processor, mix flour, ¼ c. of the butter and the white sugar until crumbly. Press into pan and bake 10 minutes. In saucepan heat remaining butter, brown sugar, and honey until melted and bubbly. Boil 1 minute. Stir in cream and nuts. Pour over crust; bake an additional 20 minutes or until it is bubbly. Cool; lift foil out of pan and cut into diamond shapes.

Bread Pudding

Heat 3 C milk   1 ½ T melted butter
mix in 2 C soft bread cubes

Mix :

¾ C sugar	⅓ t salt
½ cup raisins	½ C coconut
3 beaten eggs.	

Add to milk mixture.
Pour into greased quart casserole baking dish; place casserole in a pan of hot water. Bake at 350 degrees for 1 hour or until set.

Cinnamon Bread Pudding

4 ¼ C cinnamon bread, cubed	4 eggs beaten
2 ½ C half and half	½ C sugar
1 t vanilla extract	1 C whipped cream
Black berries	

Preheat oven to 350 degrees. Place bread in greased 13x9 pan. Combine eggs, milk sugar and vanilla in a bowl. Pour over bread. Bake 40 minutes. Or until a knife inserted near center comes out clean. Serve warm with whipped cream and black berries.

Anney's Bread Pudding

1 ¼ C sugar, divided	¼ C butter
½ t cinnamon	8 large eggs, lightly beaten
⅓ C raisins	1 qt half and half
1 vanilla bean	1 pint sweetened, whipped cream
1 loaf day old Chalah or other egg bread cubed	

Grease a 13 X 9" pan. Mix ¼ C sugar and cinnamon in cup. Toss bread, melted butter, raisins, and cinnamon/sugar mixture in large bowl to coat bread. Spread in prepared pan. Whisk eggs in large bowl. In saucepan, heat milk, remaining sugar and vanilla bean to boil over medium heat. Remove vanilla bean and scrape out seeds. Add to milk mixture. Carefully mix eggs into hot milk mixture; pour over bread. Place 13 X 9 pan in large roasting pan. Add hot water to roasting pan to create water bath for pudding. Place pans in 400 degree oven and bake for 35 – 40 minutes until custard is set. Cool on wire rack and serve with dollop of whipped cream.

New Recipes

$\mathscr{B}$reads and $\mathscr{P}$astries

❧❦

One of the best smells on earth is baking bread. We know realtors use smell to entice feelings of hominess. They often can be found baking cookies in model homes or at open houses. We think home sales might double if they would switch to bread! We love a good cookie, but we would choose bread over cookies any day. We love to go to New York just for the breads and pastries. It is a bonus that Kailee goes to school there, but don't tell her we go for the food!

<u>Danish Pastry and Fillings</u>

2 pkg. Yeast	1 c. butter
¼ c. water	3 eggs, beaten
¾ c. milk heated	4 ½ c. flour
1 tsp salt	

Sprinkle yeast on ¼ cup of warm water, stir and let stand a few minutes. Pour hot milk over 1/3 c. sugar, salt and ¼ c. butter. Cool to lukewarm. Add yeast, eggs, stir in flour and place dough in a greased 9x13 pan cover with plastic wrap. Chill 1 – 2 hours.

Let ¾ c. butter come to room temperature. Then blend in ¼ c. flour. Spread on wax paper to 10 x 12 rectangle. Cover and set aside until ½ hour before rolling dough – then refrigerate.

Roll dough to 12 x 20 rectangle; remove top cover from butter, cover lower 2/3 of dough, remove top paper. Fold down unbuttered third of dough, then over it fold remaining 1/3 so you have dough-butter-dough-butter-dough.

Roll into 10x18 rectangle; sprinkle with flour if butter breaks thru.
Fold into 1/3 again, refrigerate 10 minutes. Repeat rolling-folding-chilling two more times. Place back in pan, cover and refrigerate overnight.

SPANDAUERS –
Roll ½ of dough to ¼ inch thickness. Let relax 2-3 minutes. Cut into 3-inch squares and put filling (1 tsp) in center and fold corners into center. Put on baking sheet and push down slightly on center. Let rise 20 minutes. Brush with egg glaze. Bake at 425 for 10 minutes. Reduce heat to 375 and bake until golden brown.

CRESENTS –
Cut rolled dough into 5 ½ inch strips. Cut in 3 inch triangles. Place 1 tsp filling at base, roll up from base; put on baking sheet, point under. Let rise, glaze and bake same as #1

SNAILS –
Roll dough, cut into long 12" strips. Twist, and then coil into snail shape. Tuck end under. Let rise, put small amount of filling in center. Glaze, bake, cool, frost and sprinkle with chopped nuts.

BEAR CLAWS –
Roll dough to ½ inch thickness, 25 inches long. Let rest 5 minutes. Cut into 2 ½ inch wide strips and then roll strips again so they are 3 inches wide. Put a narrow length of romonce and one of almond filling down length of dough. Fold 1/3 of dough over filling. Brush remaining 1/3 with egg wash and fold over first; press lightly, then turn over and cut into 2 ½ inch lengths. Place on baking sheet, slash each piece 3-4 times, and brush with egg. Sprinkle with ground almond and sugar. Let rise and bake.

COFFEE CAKE – FRUIT AND OR CHEESE –
Roll 1/3 dough into a 6-inch wide, ¼ inch thick rectangle. Cover center 1/3 with cream cheese filling and then fruit filling. Cut outside edge in ½ inch strips. Fold cut pieces over center. Let rise. Glaze and bake. OR Roll ¼ of dough into a 10x12 ¼ inch thick rectangle, lightly spread center with almond filling; brush ends with egg wash, fold one side piece over filling. Brush other side with egg wash and fold over. Press all edges to seal. Place on baking sheet, folded sides down. With sharp knife make 5-6 diagonal cuts. Let rise and bake. Brush with frosting.

CHRISTMAS WREATH –
Roll ½ dough into 12x9 rectangle. Cut into 3 – 3x12 rectangles. Place narrow strip of almond filling down center of each strip. Bring edges over filling and pinch to seal. Repeat with other two pieces. Braid 3 pieces starting at middle. Join ends together to form wreath. Put on baking sheet and glaze; bake, cool, frost, decorate.

Egg Glaze – Beat 1 whole egg with 2 tsp water – or use leftover egg whites (1 tsp water to 1 egg white.)

<u>Fillings:</u>

<u>Remonce</u> – This is a Danish filling: Equal parts sugar and butter (1 cup of each) and ¼ tsp vanilla. Beat until smooth, store in refrigerator but use at room temperature.

<u>Almond Paste</u> – 1 ½ cups blanched almonds, 1 ½ cups powdered sugar, 1 egg white, 1 tsp almond extract. Grind almonds until fine, add rest of ingredients, makes a stiff paste. Store in refrigerator.

<u>Cheese Filling</u> – 2 T. raisins (soak in hot water 15 minutes.) Cream 8 oz. Cream cheese, ¼ c. sugar, 1 T. flour. Add 1 egg yolk, 1 T. sour cream, ½ tsp lemon rind, ½ tsp. Vanilla. Add drained raisins or not.

<u>Streusel Topping</u> – Equal amounts of flour and sugar (1/2 cup of each), and ½ as much butter (1/4 cup). Cut butter into flour and sugar to fine crumbs, use as is or add cinnamon and chopped nuts.

Valayne had a youth leader that took the time to teach a group of young girls to make cream puffs. We can't imagine how much patience she had to have to do that – well, yes we can. We still remember the great time they had. Our youth leader, Bonnie, may remember it differently. The recipe has become a favorite. We use the custard in many other recipes. It is a great basic custard filling that is so rich and great to use in other recipes.

Bonnie's Cream Puffs and Éclairs

½ C butter   1 C flour
1 C water   ¼ t salt
4 eggs

Bring butter and water to a boil. Turn heat to low and add flour and salt all at once. Stirring vigorously. Cook and stir until mixture forms a ball that doesn't separate. Remove from heat and cool slightly. Add eggs, one at a time, beating after each addition until smooth and completely incorporated.

Drop by heaping tablespoons onto greased cookie sheets. Bake at 450 for 15 minutes; then 325 for 20 minutes. Remove from oven; cut open tops, turn oven off, and place puffs back in oven to dry out – about 20 minutes. Cool on rack and fill.

Éclairs – instead of dropping by spoonfuls, pipe dough out onto cookie sheets with large piping tip in about 3" strips.

French Custard Filling
for cream puffs, poppy seed cake, or anywhere a rich vanilla pudding is called for

⅓ C sugar

1 T flour

1 T cornstarch

¼ t salt

1 ½ C milk

1 slightly beaten egg yolk

1 t vanilla

½ C whipping cream, whipped

Mix sugar, flour, cornstarch, and salt in heavy saucepan. Gradually stir in milk. Bring to boil; cook and stir 2 or 3 minutes longer. Temper egg yolk and add to mixture. Stirring constantly, return to boil. Add vanilla, cool, and then beat until smooth. Fold in whipped cream.

Cream Puff Frosting – chocolate ganache

Dash salt

½ C butter

1 t vanilla

1 lb powdered sugar

3 or 4 T cocoa powder

⅓ C milk

Heat salt, butter, vanilla, cocoa, and milk until melted. Stir in powdered sugar until thick and smooth.

❧❦

This cream puff recipe can also be altered to be a savory dish instead of a dessert. Just ad some cheese and herbs to the cream puff recipe and fill with your favorite chicken, tuna, shrimp, or lobster salad. Make little mini puffs or larger rounds depending on the occasion.

Baklava

1 C sugar

1 C butter

1 ½ t cinnamon

1 – 16 oz. package phyllo dough

2 C chopped nuts (you can use one kind or just your favorite kind)

Preheat oven to 350 degrees. Butter the bottoms and sides of a 9x13 pan.

Chop nuts and stir them with the cinnamon and sugar. Set aside. Unroll phyllo dough. Cut stack in half to fit pan. Cover phyllo with a dampened cloth to keep from drying out as you work. Place two sheets of dough in pan butter using a pastry brush. Repeat until you have 8 sheets layered. Sprinkle with ¼ of the cinnamon, sugar and nut mixture. Repeat this process until you use all the mix and all the phyllo; ending with phyllo on top.

Using a sharp knife cut into diamond or square shapes all the way to the bottom of the pan. Bake for about 50 minutes until baklava is golden and crisp.

Make sauce while baklava is baking:

1 C water

1 t vanilla

½ C honey

1 C white sugar

1 T lemon juice

Boil sugar, water and lemon until sugar is melted. Add vanilla and honey. Simmer for about 20 minutes.

Remove baklava from oven and immediately spoon sauce over it. Let cool. This freezes well. Leave it uncovered, as it gets soggy if it is wrapped up.

❧❦

This makes a great breakfast treat. It makes a fabulous dessert too. You can double this recipe and it fits nicely into a sheet pan. It is just as easy to make for a crowd and share as it is to make a single recipe for your family. It is yummy warm, but serves up prettier if you let it cool and set for a few minutes. We have never taken this treat anywhere – whether for a dessert or breakfast – and not had people begging for the recipe.

Cheese Squares

2 – 8oz cans of crescent rolls   1 C sugar
2 – 8oz pkgs cream cheese   ½ t vanilla
1 egg yolk   1 C powdered sugar
2-4 T evaporated milk

Press one package of rolls into a 9X13" pan. Cream cheese and sugar together; add egg and flavoring. Spread mixture on top of rolls. Press other package of rolls onto waxed paper the size and shape of 9X13" pan. Turn over to top cheese mixture. Bake at 350 degrees for 30 minutes. Mix milk and powdered sugar together to make glaze. Spread glaze over squares when warm from the oven. Cool and refrigerate until set. Cut into squares. This recipe fits nicely into a cookie sheet when doubled.

Cream Puffs in a Pan

Crust:
1 cube + 2 T. Margarine   1 ¼ C water
Bring to a boil and remove from heat. Add:
1 ¼ C flour
Stir into a ball with a wooden spoon. Cool for 5 minutes. Stir in:
5 eggs
One at a time, stirring until completely incorporated into the dough. Spread crust into a greased cookie sheet. Bake at 400 degrees for 15-18 minutes. Cool completely and spread on filling.

Filling:
1 – 8oz package cream cheese   3 ½ C milk
1 large box of vanilla instant pudding
Blend ingredients in a blender until thick and smooth. Spread on crust.

Frosting:
1 – 8 oz frozen whipped topping
1 can chocolate frosting

Stir whipped topping and spread over filling. In a pastry tube apply chocolate frosting in a stippling design over whipped topping. Refrigerate until ready to serve.

Crepes

1 ½ C milk   1 C flour
3 eggs   ½ t salt
2 t melted butter

Beat all ingredients in bowl and place in refrigerator 1 hour or overnight. Pour ¼ C batter in heated crepe pan or non-stick frying pan heated. Cook until set. Fill with sweet or savory filling.

❧✿

This crepe recipe can also be used in savory dishes instead of for dessert. Add some cheese and herbs and stuff with your favorite meats and cheeses. For a really great dinner, fill some savory crepes with cooked chicken and cheese and top with Alfredo sauce and more cheese. Bake in the oven until bubbly. Serve with a green salad and your favorite dressing and you have a dinner or lunch your family will love.

Bran Muffin Mix

Mix together and let stand:
2C Nabisco All Bran (the little buds)   2 C Boiling water

Mix together well:
2 ½ C. Sugar   1 C. Shortening

Add to sugar mixture 4 eggs one at a time until well blended. Add :
5C flour   4 t. baking soda
1 ½ t salt   bran mixture above
1 qt. buttermilk

Then add 4 C. Kellogg's All Bran (the worm looking one)

Stir by hand until mixed. Store in sealed container in fridge for up to 10 weeks. Bake in muffin tins at 350 degrees for 20 minutes. Improves with age. Do not stir again, just spoon and bake.

Basic Muffin Recipe

1 ½ C sugar	12 tablespoons (1 ½ sticks) unsalted butter, at
3 extra-large eggs, at room temperature	room temperature
8 oz sour cream	1 ½ t pure vanilla extract
2 ½ cups all-purpose flour	¼ C milk
½ t baking soda	2 t baking powder
2 half-pints fresh blueberries*	½ t kosher salt

Preheat the oven to 350 degrees F. Place 16 paper liners in muffin pans.

In the bowl of an electric mixer fitted with the paddle attachment, cream the butter and sugar until light and fluffy, about 5 minutes. With the mixer on low speed, add the eggs 1 at a time, and then add the vanilla, sour cream, and milk. In a separate bowl, sift together the flour, baking powder, baking soda, and salt. With the mixer on low speed add the flour mixture to the batter and beat until just mixed. Fold in the blueberries with a spatula and be sure the batter is completely mixed.

Scoop the batter into the prepared muffin pans, filling each cup just over the top, and bake for 25 to 30 minutes, until the muffins are lightly browned on top and a cake tester comes out clean.

⤳⤲

*Becoming a muffin master is easy. Flavor the basic muffin batter by adding, for example: 1 chopped banana and 3/4 cup semisweet chocolate chips; or 1 cup toasted almonds, 3/4 cup dried cranberries, and 1/4 teaspoon almond extract; or 1 cup chopped drained canned pineapple and 1 cup sweetened flaked coconut; or 1 cup chopped dried apricots and 1 T poppy seeds. One of the really great thing about cooking from scratch is you get to make things your own. You can add the things you like and you don't have to rely on what others think would taste great. We have tested many muffin recipes. Many of them are tasty but dry. This recipe is not only delicious but moist and easily adaptable. Blueberries freeze really well. If you live where you can pick your own and freeze them while they are in season, you can have yummy berries all year round. (If you can keep them away from your husband and kids!)

Popovers – Lynne Haley

1 C of flour	2 eggs
¼ t salt	1 C Milk
1 T butter, melted	

Sift flour and salt. Beat eggs with rotary beater, add milk, butter and sift in flour; beating only enough to make a smooth batter.

Fill iron popover pans or muffin pans, previously heated and greased, (well greased), one-third full. Bake in very hot oven, 450 degrees F. For 30 minutes, then at 350 degrees F for 15 minutes or until well risen, browned, and crusty. Do not open oven door for first 30 minutes.

This is another recipe easily adapted to your tastes or to suite a meal you are having. You can add cheeses, bacon, fruit, herbs, or whatever you can imagine to go with what you want.

Best Ever Cornbread

From Shawna

2 eggs	¾ C sugar
1c milk	½ t baking soda
¾ - 1 cube butter	3-4 heaping T cornmeal
2 c baking mixes	

Ok the recipe says to soften butter and then just mix everything together........I usually mix everything and then add the butter (melted) last. Also I generally use the whole cube of butter and the 4 full T of the corn meal. This is supposed to go in an 8x8 pan for 35 minutes. I almost always double it and make it in this bigger glass dish that I have although I am unsure of the size. I would check it at 30 minutes and then watch it very closely because I swear that one minute it will be "gooey" in the middle and then literally ONE minute later it will be TOO done.

Sistersfamilyrecipes@gmail.com

French Bread

1 T yeast	1 ½ t salt
1 ½ C very warm water	1 T olive oil
2 T sugar	4 C flour

1 egg white & 2 T. water – whisk them together

Mix yeast sugar, and water. Let stand 5 minutes. Add oil and flour; mix well. Let rise in greased bowl. Punch down every 10 minutes for 1 hour. Divide into 2 balls; let stand for 10 minutes. Roll into 9x12 rectangle, and then roll up into a loaf. Make slits on top. Let rise for 1 ½ hours on a greased cookie sheet. Brush with egg and water mixture. Bake at 400 for 25 – 30 minutes.

Easy Pita Bread

2 t active dry yeast	1 T sugar
1 ¼ C warm water (about 110 to 115°)	3 ½ C all-purpose flour
½ t salt	oil

Put yeast in ¼ C of the water; add sugar and let stand for 10 minutes. Sift 2 ½ C of flour and the salt into a warm bowl. Form a well in the center; pour in yeast mixture and remaining warm water. Begin to mix with hand, wooden spoon, or dough hook, adding remaining flour as needed. Turn out onto a floured surface and knead for about 10 to 15 minutes, until smooth and no longer sticky. Oil a large bowl; place dough in bowl and turn to coat with oil. Cover with a damp cloth and put in a warm place free of drafts for 1 ½ to 2 hours. Dough should be doubled in bulk. Knead for a few minutes then divide into balls about 2 1/2 inches in diameter. Roll balls into circles on a lightly floured surface with floured rolling pin, or flatten into circles with hand. The circles should be about 1/4-inch thick and about 7 inches in diameter. Sandwich the circles between floured cloths and let rise for about 20 minutes in a warm place. Preheat oven to 475°. Sprinkle cookie sheets with flour or oil. Place loaves on baking sheets and bake 5 to 10 minutes. If baking sheets are oiled, turn pita loaves to brown both sides. Remove to wire racks to cool.

We don't have a family dinner or get together without these rolls. They are delicious and never fail. Adjust the sugar to your taste – some of us use a little less. The roll dough is great for cinnamon rolls and other recipes that call for sweet dough. The best part of making these is that the cook gets to taste one (or more) hot out of the oven. There are few things better!

Paula's Rolls

3 C warm water	4 eggs beaten
2 C sugar	1 T salt
1 cube butter	2 T shortening
3 T yeast	

Dissolve yeast in 1 cup of the water plus 1 T of the sugar. Melt butter and shortening and add remaining 2 cups of the water, add eggs, sugar and salt. Then add the yeast mixture; stir well. Stir in 8 cups of flour; it will make a sticky dough*. Let rise 2 hours and punch down; let rise again for 2 additional hours. Divide in half and roll each half into a rectangle; cut in circles and dip into melted butter and fold in half (butter side in) and place on cookie sheet. Recipe will fill 2 cookie sheets and makes about 5 dozen rolls. Let rise to desired size (about 2 hours.) Bake at 300 degrees for 25 – 30 minutes.

*You can also cover them after mixing the dough and place in the fridge overnight.

Beth's 24-hour Butterhorns

1 C lukewarm water	¼ C sugar
1 T yeast	½ C butter
3 eggs, beaten	4 C flour

Place water in large bowl. Add sugar and sprinkle in yeast. Add melted butter, eggs, salt and flour. Stir to mix well; cover and let rise 3-6 hours or overnight in fridge. Divide in half and roll each half into a circle 1/8" thick. Brush with butter and cut into 16 pie-shaped wedges. Roll up from large end to point and place on greased cookie sheet. Let rise 4-6 hours or until tripled in size. Bake at 350 degrees for 10 minutes.

Bread

This recipe is from our good friend Vida Hatch. I don't think she ever bought any bread! She made the best bread ever and used to make hundreds of loaves as gifts at Christmas time.

Heat to lukewarm:

1 ½ qts. Milk	3 cubes butter

Combine in bowl and let stand about 5 minutes:

1 ½ C warm water	¼ C sugar
4 T yeast	

Measure into large pan:

4 t salt	8-10 eggs
2 C honey	

Add yeast mixture and milk mixture. Add about 8 C whole wheat flour a little at a time. Stir with fork until too hard to stir by hand, and then knead in pan. Add enough white flour to make a good, smooth, dough. Let rise about 1 ½ hours. Punch down and put into loaf pans; let rise and bake at 300 degrees for 40 minutes.

Aunt Sylvia's Soft, Light, Yummy, Whole Wheat Bread

10 C Hard white wheat flour	1 t Salt
2 T Lecithin	¼ C gluten
2 T Yeast	2 T Dough Enhancer
⅔ C Honey	5 C Hot water

Sift flour and add other dry ingredients. Add honey and hot water. Start mixer and add additional flour until dough starts climbing out of bowl. Knead for 5 minutes. Place dough on oiled bread board and divide into 4 equal pieces. (Oil hands to avoid sticking to hands.) Shape dough into loaves and place in greased loaf pans. Place in oven. Cover with clean cotton cloth.

Turn oven on to 350 degrees for 30 seconds then turn oven off. Let dough rise in warm oven for 45 minutes. Bake at 345 degrees for 25 minutes. Butter or grease tops of hot bread. Enjoy. Freezes very well.

Maori Bread
From our good friend Linda Wisheart who could make this bread in her sleep.

1 C sugar	2 T yeast
4 C lukewarm water	6 C flour

Mix with wire whip in medium size bowl and let sit for 20 minutes.

Pour into a large bowl and make a hole in the middle. Pour yeast mixture in the center. Mix until it forms soft dough. Let stand for 20 minutes.

Split into 3 loaves. Place in greased pans. Let stand for 20 – 25 minutes. Bake in 350 degree oven for 45 minutes. It is easy to make and it taste divine. It makes the best peanut butter and jelly sandwiches and yummy toast.

Knotted Rolls
Mix the following until warm before adding eggs:

¾ C margarine	1 C instant potato flakes
¾ C sugar	1 T salt
2 C flour	

Then add:

4 eggs, whipped	1 T yeast
6 C flour	3 C milk (scalding hot)

Combine and knead until smooth and elastic. Place in bowl and let rise 1 hour. Divide dough in half. Roll into rectangle and spread with melted butter or filling (below). Fold dough into thirds to encase filling and make 3 layers. Cut into 12 strips and twist into knots. Place on cookie sheets and let rise 2-3 hours. Bake at 375 for 10 minutes.

Fillings: After spreading with butter you can add one of the following or keep plain

Orange	Cinnamon
½ C sugar	¾ C sugar
grated rind from 2 oranges	¾ C brown sugar
	1 T ground cinnamon

Glaze:	Glaze:
4-5 C powdered sugar	4-5 C powdered sugar
⅓ C orange juice	½ t vanilla
1 ½ T vanilla	3 T milk

⊰⊱

This bread is beautiful as well as delicious. At Easter we have made it with colored eggs woven into the braid before baking. It makes a beautiful centerpiece as well as bread for the dinner. You can hard cooked eggs or raw. You can use colored eggs or white. Shape the braid into a circle and place the eggs in the loosely braided dough. It is really very pretty.

Finnish Braid

5 – 5 ⅓ C flour
2 pkgs active dry yeast (4 t)
½ t ground cardamom
1 C milk
½ C butter
½ C sugar

1 t salt
2 eggs
1 T finely shredded orange peel
⅓ C orange juice
1 egg yolk
1 T milk

In large mixer bowl combine 2 C flour, yeast, and cardamom. In saucepan, heat the 1 C milk, butter, sugar, and salt to just warm (115 degrees). Add to flour mixture in mixing bowl; add 2 eggs, orange peel and orange juice. Beat at low speed for ½ minute or so scraping sides then 3 minutes on high. Stir in as much of the remaining flour as you can mix in by hand.

Turn onto floured surface and knead in enough of the remaining flour to make moderately soft dough. Continue kneading until smooth and elastic. (5-8 minutes). Place in greased bowl; turn. Cover and let rise in warm place until double – about 1 hour. Punch down.

Divide in half. Divide each half into thirds. Shape into 6 balls and roll into ropes of even lengths. Braid loosely beginning in the middle and working your way out to each end. Pinch ends together. Cover and let rise about 30 minutes.

Stir together egg yolk and 1 T milk. Brush braids with egg mixture and bake at 350 degrees for 25-30 minutes.

Rosemary Focaccia Bread

This quick and easy bread is perfect for just about any meal, but especially good with any pasta or Italian dish. It also makes a great base for sandwiches especially paninis

2 t sugar	6 T plus 1 teaspoon extra-virgin olive oil
3 envelopes (3/4 ounce) active dry yeast	2 C warm water (about 110 degrees F.)
5 1/2 C flour (or more as needed)	3 t fine salt
1 T chopped fresh rosemary	1 t kosher salt
1 head roasted garlic	1 onion caramelized in olive oil
Cracked pepper	Shredded cheese (optional)
Other herbs (optional)	

Lightly oil a large bowl with 1 teaspoon of the oil and set aside.

In a blender combine onions, garlic and 2 tablespoons of olive oil. Blend until liquified.

In a large mixing bowl, combine the yeast, sugar, water, and oil and onion mixture, stir and let sit until foamy, about 5 minutes. Add the flour and salt, and mix on low speed until the dough comes together and forms a ball – about 2 to 3 minutes. Increase the speed to medium and mix for 8 minutes. If the dough is still sticky, continue mixing and gradually add the remaining 1/4 cup flour.

Form into a ball and place in the prepared bowl. Cover with plastic wrap or a kitchen towel, and let rest in a warm, draft-free place until doubled in size, 1 to 1 1/2 hours. Preheat the oven to 400 degrees F.

Grease a 9 by 13-inch baking sheet with 1 tablespoon of the olive oil. Turn the dough out onto the baking sheet, pressing evenly across the bottom of the pan. Cover with plastic wrap and set in a warm, draft-free place until it rises until nearly doubled, 30 minutes to 1 hour. With your fingertips, make dimples in the dough. Drizzle with the remaining 3 tablespoons of oil and sprinkle with the rosemary, pepper, and kosher salt. Bake on the lower oven rack until just golden brown, 25 to 30 minutes.

This bread can be modified with shredded cheese on top, other herbs on top, leaving out the onions and garlic, etc.

Amish Friendship Bread

Combine in a large non-metal bowl:

1 C flour   1 C sugar
1 C milk

Stir thoroughly and pour into zip top bag.

Day 1 this is the day you receive the bag or make the mix – do nothing
Day 2 mush the bag
Day 3 mush the bag
Day 4 mush the bag
Day 5 mush the bag
Day 6 add 1 C flour, 1 C sugar, 1 C milk and mush the bag
Day 7 mush the bag
Day 8 mush the bag
Day 9 mush the bag
Day 10 make the bread

Combine in a large non-metal bowl combine:

the batter from zip top bag,   1 C sugar
1 C milk

Stir and divide into zip top bags. Fill 4 zip top bags with 1 C of batter. Give 3 to a friend and keep one to use. To remaining batter add:

1 C oil   3 eggs
2 C flour   1 C sugar
½ C milk   1 t vanilla
2 t cinnamon   ½ t baking soda
½ t salt   1 ½ t baking powder
1 large box of instant vanilla pudding

Pour into two greased loaf pans dusted with sugar and cinnamon. Sprinkle top with cinnamon and sugar. Bake at 325 for one hour. Cool ten minutes and remove from pan.

Pizza Dough

1 T. yeast	1 c. warm water
¼ c. olive oil	1 tsp. sugar
½ tsp salt	2 ½ c. flour

Dissolve yeast in warm water in large bowl. Stir in oil, sugar, salt and 2 c. flour; stir until smooth. Turn dough onto floured surface kneading in enough of remaining flour to make dough easy to handle. Place into greased bowl; turn over once and let rise about 45 min. Press into cookie sheet and top as desired.

෴

This is a family favorite of our Aunt Sylvia. Her family enjoys this bread for Thanksgiving and Christmas every year and any time they feel like having some great bread. We rarely have a Sunday dinner or family get together without some kind of homemade bread or rolls. The cook gets to eat the first one hot and fresh from the oven!

Monkey Bread

2 C warm water	7 C flour
½ C sugar	4 T melted shortening
2 T yeast	1 T salt
2 eggs	2 cubes butter

Mix water, sugar, and yeast; set aside. Beat eggs and add to mixture. Sift 3 C flour and beat into mixture. Add melted shortening. Sift remaining 4 C of flour. Stir flour and salt into mixture. Keep sifting until well mixed. Cover with a damp towel. Let rise until doubled. Stir down, cover and refrigerate overnight. About two hours before planning to eat, melt each cube of butter and put one melted cube in each of two bundt pans. Roll out dough to ½" thick. Cut with a regular size jar lid. Let rise. Divide cut dough into 2 portions. Place dough pieces on their sides around the inside of each bundt pan. Bake at 400 degrees for 20 minutes.

Grandma Nina's Orange Rolls

2 packages of yeast	½ C warm water
¼ C sugar	
mix and set aside to activate	

6 C flour	½ C powdered milk
1 T salt	2 beaten eggs
½ C melted shortening	2 ¼ C warm water

Mix all together, then add yeast mixture. Let rise, punch down and rise again. Roll out, spread with orange sauce.

Orange Sauce

½ C fresh squeezed orange juice	1 T orange zest
1 ½ C sugar	1 cube butter

Place in sauce pan, bring to boil; cook 7 minutes stirring constantly (after it comes to boil) let cool and spread on dough, roll, slice and place in muffin tin (to keep the sauce in) bake at 350 degrees 12-18 minutes or until light brown.

Pumpkin Bread

3 c. sugar	3 ½ c. flour
1 c. oil	3 tsp soda
4 eggs	1 ½ tsp salt
2/3 c. water	1 ½ tsp cinnamon
2 c. pumpkin	1 tsp nutmeg
	2/3 c. nuts

Mix thoroughly pour into 3 large greased and floured loaf pans. Bake at 350 for 1 hour until done.

ॐ◌ॐ

This is the best banana bread ever! My mom has made this for years. It is what my youngest daughter wants me to bring her every time we come visit her at school. I haven't met anyone I've shared this with who didn't love it. If you buy fruit, you usually have a banana or two that gets over ripe before you can eat it. Take the peel off, pop it in a freezer zip top bag, and save up three of them for this recipe.

Banana Bread

½ C oil   3 very ripe bananas mashed
2 eggs   ½ t salt
1 C sugar   1 t vanilla
½ t baking powder   ½ t baking soda
2 C flour   chopped nuts

Beat eggs and sugar until smooth; add oil and mix well. Add all other ingredients and pour into two loaf pans. Bake at 350 for 60 minutes.

New Recipes

Main Dishes

We come from a long line of creative cooks. My Great-Grandpa Gulley had the best meatloaf recipe in the world. He added ground ham to keep the meatloaf moist and flavorful. My Grandma McGee lived during the depression and had to be creative to feed her three daughters. My mom had four very picky eaters to contend with. She experimented a lot in the kitchen and taught all of us to make just about everything from scratch. Frozen dinners were a rare treat and I don't remember having boxed mixes around.

I didn't appreciate the quality and care that went into our "home-made" cooking when I was a child. I just remember feeling like the only kid that didn't bring a package of store-bought cookies to school. Mine were always on a plate, fresh from the oven. It is still cheaper to make your own cookies, but they also taste so much better! That could be said for almost anything. Just try the meatloaf! We also know what goes into everything we eat. We have made it ourselves. We have also taste tested every recipe, made changes as we found something that worked better or tasted better, and tasted them again.

Café Rio Pork
Pork:

3 lbs pork butt or shoulder roast   1 ½ c. ketchup

20 oz. Coca Cola   1 clove garlic, minced

Sauce:

2 c. tomatillo sauce   salt & pepper

1 ½ c. brown sugar   1 tsp garlic powder

Juice of 2 limes

Place pork in crock pot. Stir together cola and ketchup. Add minced garlic. Pour over meat. Cook on high 4 to 6 hours. When pork is tender, shred and place back in crock pot. Combine the sauce ingredients and pour over pork. Cook on low one hour. Take lid off to thicken mixture.

Ranch dressing for pork salad:

1 c. milk   3 T dry Ranch dressing mix

1 c. mayonnaise   1 can diced green chilies

Put all ingredients for dressing in blender. Blend until smooth. Refrigerate.

Costa Vida Sweet Pork
3 lb. Pork roast   1 can El Pato

1 can Dr. Pepper   2 c. brown sugar

1 can green chilies   ½ pkg. Fajita seasoning

1 tsp garlic powder

Place pork roast in crockpot. Fill halfway with water. Cook on high 5 hours. Take pork out of crockpot and shred. Drain the liquid. Place shredded pork back in crockpot. Puree salsa, green chilies, fajita seasoning and garlic powder. Add Dr. Pepper and brown sugar and mix. Pour over meat and cook on low for a few hours until fully marinated.

Manicotti

Meat filling:

½ lb ground beef	2 links hot Italian Sausage (cut out of casing)
1 t garlic minced	2 links sweet Italian Sausage (cut out of casing)
1 C ricotta cheese	½ lb grated mozzarella
½ t. salt	½ C mayonnaise

Sauce:

2 Large. Cans tomato sauce	1 tsp Oregano
1 tsp garlic minced	½ tsp basil
½ tsp rosemary	½ lb grated mozzarella

Brown hamburger, sausage and garlic; drain. Mix ricotta, mozzarella salt and mayo., refrigerate until ready to use. Boil 14-16 manicotti until tender; drain and add cold water. Remove from water one at a time. Stuff with cheese and meat mixture. Lay in a 9x13 pan. Put all sauce ingredients except ½ lb. grated mozzarella in a sauce pan and simmer for ½ hour. Pour over the top of the manicotti and then sprinkle mozzarella cheese over the top. Bake at 350 degrees for 25 – 30 minutes.

Smooth Spaghetti Sauce

– I have kids with texture issues! They did not like spaghetti sauce with any "chunks" in it. I came up with one that tastes great that I use over pasta and to make lasagna with. You can also put all ingredients in the crock pot and cook overnight or all day and have great sauce ready for you without much work at all.

1 lb ground beef	2 cloves garlic
1 – 28oz can tomato sauce	1 – 28 oz can tomato puree
1 large can tomato paste	2 t dried basil
1 t dried oregano	3 T sugar

Brown ground beef in a little olive oil and 1 clove of minced garlic in large saucepan. Add all other ingredients. Turn heat to low, cover pot, and let simmer for at least 30 minutes. It is even better if you can simmer for several hours. The sauce is best made the day before, but can be used right away.

Sistersfamilyrecipes@gmail.com

Chalupas

This is a great burrito or soft taco filling when you are cooking for a large group. Set out tortillas, lettuce, chopped tomatoes, onions, guacamole, cheese, salsa, and sour cream and let everyone make their own custom burrito.

½ lb pinto beans (dry)	½ lb black beans (dry)
5 lbs roast (pork or beef)	1 can El pato hot sauce
2 cloves garlic	1 T. cumin
1 tsp Oregano	2 Hatch green chilies (whole)
1 T salt	

Cover with water in a roaster and cook until done. Pull the roast apart and stir.

7-Day Brisket

1 bottle liquid smoke	garlic powder
onion powder	season salt
pepper	3-5 lb brisket
1 bottle of your favorite bar-b-q sauce	¼ c. Worcestershire sauce

Day 1 – season brisket with garlic, onion, season salt, and pepper. Put in a large Zip bag. Pour in ½ bottle of liquid smoke. Put in the refrigerator.
Day 2 – Turn the bag over and moosh it around.
Day 3 – Add the Worcestershire sauce and the rest of the liquid smoke.
Day 4 – Add more of the garlic, onion, season salt and pepper.
Day 5 – In the morning: Turn the bag over and moosh it around. That night: Wrap the meat in foil and put it in a pan, cook it overnight at 250 degrees.
Day 6 – Let the meat cool; slice it thin and place it in a baking dish. Cover it with foil and refrigerate overnight.
Day 7 – Pour Bar-B-Q sauce over sliced meat. Bake at 350 degrees until hot. Serve.

❧

If you want the best brisket you may ever eat in your life and you want to eat it in less than a week before you start the process – although the above recipe is really good – you might enjoy this recipe for Texas Brisket from our friend Cindy. She is famous for her brisket, chili and carrot cake. She is not originally from Texas, but she loved to tell everyone that she got there as quick as she could! The brisket recipes are quite similar with the major difference being time. The time is worth the investment for either recipe. Brisket says summer just like burgers cooked out on a grill. Just add potato salad and corn on the cob and you are all set for the perfect summer lunch or dinner.

Texas Brisket

1 Whole beef brisket	1 t garlic salt
2 cloves garlic	1 t onion salt
1 bottle liquid smoke	1 t grill seasoning

Put meat and seasonings in an extra large zip top bag and refrigerate several hours – best overnight. Take out brisket and bring to room temperature. Place in foil along with juices and seal well. Place foil wrapped meat on cookie sheet or in baking dish and bake at 325 for 6 hours. Remove from oven, remove meat and place in baking dish; cover with your favorite BBQ sauce – we like Bull's eye – and bake for another 30 minutes unwrapped. Remove. Let stand for about 10 minutes. Slice brisket against the grain and serve with beans, corn on the cob, potato salad, and rolls.

Bar-B-Q Sauce

1 ½ C brown sugar	½ C black pepper
1 ½ C mustard	½ C red pepper flakes
1 qt Catsup	1 ½ C salt
1 Qt white wine	2 Qt water
3 Qt red wine vinegar	1 ½ C Worcestershire sauce

Combine all ingredients and let flavors blend overnight. Store in airtight container.

Kalua Pork

3 – 5 lbs pork shoulder or butt
1 tsp. Liquid Smoke
a few sprinkles of sea salt
On heavy duty Aluminum Foil center roast. Sprinkle salt and Liquid Smoke. Wrap Roast up tightly and then wrap it again. Cook overnight at 250. With rubber gloves on remove the fat and pull the meat apart. Serve.

Our mom is a pretty creative cook with a very discerning pallet – that is code for "picky eater." She had the challenge of cooking for four girls with very picky eating habits and usually with a very limited budget. Time was also a factor, as it is with most busy moms. She came up with some pretty amazing recipes, that fed a crowd, on a very tight food budget. Many of these recipes have a Mexican flare and have become family favorites. Apparently one of the secrets for stretching her food budget was how little we four girls ate. One of our mom's favorite stories is the four of us sharing two hamburgers on the rare occasion we went out for fast food. Valayne ate the bun and Kerri would eat the patty.

Flat Enchiladas

This is a quick and simple version of the traditional rolled enchilada.

1 dozen corn tortillas	2 cans enchilada sauce
2 cans tomato sauce	1 lb lean ground beef, browned
thinly sliced iceberg lettuce	1 clove garlic
1 t cumin	pinch red pepper flakes
Sour cream	diced tomatoes
2 C Shredded cheese	

Heat corn tortillas in a skillet with a small amount of oil, one at a time, just until soft; set aside. Brown ground beef in skillet with garlic and cumin; add sauces and red pepper flakes. Bring to boil. Place softened tortillas one at a time in the sauce mixture; turn to coat. Scoop tortilla with some sauce and meat and place onto plate. Layer 3-4 tortillas with sauce on each plate. Top with cheese, shredded lettuce, sour cream, and diced tomatoes.

Mom's Famous Meatloaf

1 lb (not too lean) ground beef	1 lb (or more) ground ham
1 C crushed saltine crackers	1 egg
1 C tomato sauce	Chopped onion (optional)

Pepper, season salt, garlic, cajun spice (whatever you like)

Mix all ingredients together and shape into a loaf in a baking pan or roaster. Pour over the top the following:

1 C tomato sauce mixed with 2 tsp. Kitchen Bouquet and 1 cup water. You may also top with sliced onion that can be removed by picky eaters.
Bake at 350 degrees for 1 hour.

⤞⤝

Every year our little town celebrates "Gilbert Days." It is a pretty big celebration and has certainly grown over the years. Even after we were married with kids of our own, we sisters would try to make it to the Gilbert Days celebration. Mom would always have a big pot of red chili with all the fixings at home. Everyone was invited to make burritos for lunch or whenever you got hungry. We had red chili at other times too, but always for Gilbert Days. It is a quick and easy overnight dinner!

Red Chili
1 boneless roast   1 can El Pato (Mexican tomato sauce)
1 C water   2 t red pepper flakes
Season with garlic powder, pepper, salt

Place ingredients in crockpot and cook overnight or until meat falls apart. Remove meat and shred and remove any fat. Pour cooking liquid into small saucepan and thicken with flour and water mixture or cornstarch and water. Return meat to crockpot and pour enough of the liquid over meat to make a moist filling. Serve in flour tortillas, cheese, sour cream, and/or guacamole.

Green Chili
The base for this recipe is from my Aunt Sylvia, which we modified slightly.
1 small pork roast and one small beef roast (about 2 1/2 lbs. each)
1 clove garlic   2 t cumin
1 whole onion   1 t red pepper flakes
salt and pepper

Cover with beef stock and cook in crock-pot until tender; let cool. Remove onion, any remaining juices, and pull apart.

Add 1 can chopped green chilies and 1 bottle of 505 Green Chili sauce
Simmer until ready to use.

❧❧

This next recipe was the start of a new level of cooking in our home. Valayne wanted to invite her boyfriend over for a home-cooked meal to impress him. She was bored with the things we made all the time. Our mom was a great cook, but it seemed like we had the same things all the time (We often feel that way now in our own homes!) Valayne asked our mom what she could cook that would be fun and different and she handed Valayne the well-used, red checkered cookbook we had at home. Valayne leafed through the pages until she found something that sounded sophisticated and fun. The result has become a family staple and the beginning of trying and creating new recipes! Valayne likes to think our cooking revolution all started with her. This recipe also makes Thanksgiving turkey leftovers a treat!

Chicken Tetrazini

¼ C butter	¼ C flour
½ t salt	¼ t pepper
1 C chicken broth	2 cloves garlic
1 C heavy cream	1 lb thin spaghetti cooked and drained
1 pkg fresh mushrooms sliced	2 – 3 boneless chicken breasts or whole roasted chicken

In large skillet, cook chicken in olive oil with one clove garlic crushed. Set aside. Add a couple T of butter to the same pan, the other clove of garlic (diced) and the mushrooms. Cook until tender. Remove from pan. In same pan, melt the butter and add flour. Cook until bubbly. Add chicken broth and cream. Stir and cook until thick and bubbly. Add mushrooms and cubed chicken back to the sauce. Mix in cooked spaghetti and pour into greased 9 X 13 pan. Top with grated parmesan cheese and bake at 350 degrees for about 30 minutes. Serve with garlic toast.

You can use with left over roasted chicken or turkey. This is great to use up your left over Thanksgiving turkey.

Roasted Butternut Squash and Penne

2 lb cubed, roasted butternut squash

1 C goat cheese

½ C chopped basil

1 lb penne pasta cooked and drained

1 C chopped nuts

⅓ C grated parmesan cheese

Cube a peeled and seeded butternut squash. Place on baking sheet, sprinkle with salt and pepper and roast in a 440 degree oven for 30-40 minutes – until squash takes on some color. Remove and set aside to cool. Drain cooked pasta and place in large mixing bowl with goat cheese and basil. Toss until cheese is melted and incorporated. Stir in butternut squash, nuts, and sprinkle with cheese.

Chicken, Rice, and Grape Pilaf

1 Clove garlic

2 T vegetable oil

½ t sugar

½ C dry white wine

salt and pepper

8 boneless, skinless chicken thighs

½ t ground cinnamon

1 C long-grain white rice

1 ½ c chicken broth

½ C fresh parsley chopped

Thinly slice onion and mince garlic. Heat oil and add chicken and sauté until lightly browned. Add cinnamon, sugar, and garlic and sauté for a few seconds. Add rice, wine, and chicken broth; season with salt and pepper. Add chicken back to the pan and bring liquid to a simmer. Cover the pan and bake for 1 hour on 375 degrees. Slice grapes in half add them to pan and top with parsley before serving.

Company Chicken

4 – 6 boneless, skinless, chicken breasts

1 can cream of chicken soup

salt and pepper

1 bottle Italian dressing

1 – 8oz cream cheese

cooked rice or wide egg noodles

Place chicken and dressing in large zip top bag and marinate overnight or all day. Place chicken, dressing, soup, cheese, and, salt and pepper in crock pot on high and cook until chicken shreds easily. Shred meat and stir to incorporate all ingredients. Serve over hot rice or noodles.

Sistersfamilyrecipes@gmail.com

Cream Cheese Chicken

This is another version of Company Chicken from Valayne's daughter Kristal. We love chicken thighs, so we tried it and it is every bit as good as the recipe above. We leave out the onion (our families has issues with actual onions. We love the flavor, but the texture is a problem.) We substitute onion powder.

4 lbs boneless, skinless chicken thighs	2 t butter or margarine, melted
½ t black pepper	½ t salt
1 large onion, chopped	1 oz package powdered Italian salad
2 T chicken broth	dressing mix
8 ounces of cream cheese, cubed	1 can condensed cream of chicken soup
2 cloves of garlic, minced	½ C chicken broth

Brush chicken with butter and layer in crock pot, sprinkling dry Italian seasoning mix over each layer. Cook and cover on LOW for 6 to 7 hours.

About 45 minutes before done, brown the onion in the 2 t chicken broth and then add the cream cheese, soup, salt, and pepper and 1/2 cup chicken broth to the saucepan. Add the minced garlic and stir all ingredients until smooth. Pour sauce mixture over chicken in crock pot and cook an additional 30 to 45 minutes. Remove chicken to platter and stir sauce before putting into gravy bowl.

You can serve this alone with veggies, over mashed potatoes, over rice, or over noodles. It is delicious!

Chef William's Chicken with Goat Cheese & Sun-dried Tomatoes

1 T minced garlic	1 T minced onion
2 T butter	¼ C fresh lemon juice
2/3 C cold butter, sliced	1 ½ C chopped sun-dried tomatoes
¼ chopped basil	½ t kosher salt
½ t white pepper	6 boneless, skinless, chicken breasts
olive oil, for brushing	8 oz goat cheese, room temperature
½ t salt	½ t pepper
½ C wine	

Sauté garlic and onion in 2 T butter in a large skillet over medium heat until tender. Stir wine and lemon juice into skillet, increase heat to medium high, and simmer to reduce by half. Reduce heat to low and stir in cold butter, one slice at a time. Stir in tomatoes, basil, kosher salt, and white pepper; remove from heat; set aside. Brush chicken breasts with olive oil and sprinkle with salt and black pepper. Grill chicken over hot coals 15-20 minutes, or until cooked through. A couple of minutes before chicken is done, place equal amounts of cheese on each breast. Spoon prepared sun-dried tomato sauce over chicken.

Chef William's Chicken Pasta
Chicken:

6 chicken breasts, skinned & boned
½ C extra virgin olive oil
Salt & fresh ground pepper to taste

6 t balsamic vinegar
¼ C fresh basil leaves

Sauce and Pasta:

3 T butter
2 C cream
1 C frozen peas
1 (9 oz.) pkg. fresh fettuccine

4 med. shallots
6 oz. fresh mushrooms
Salt & fresh ground pepper to taste
2 oz. fresh grated Parmesan cheese

Cut breasts in half and place side by side on a platter. Drizzle with the vinegar and oil. Cut basil leaves and sprinkle over the breasts; sprinkle salt and pepper. Refrigerate at least 1 hour. Grill the breasts or bake in a 350 degree oven for 30 minutes. Set aside. Peel and finely chop shallots. Sauté in butter 1 minute. Add cream, salt and pepper to taste. Boil to reduce slightly to the consistency of a light sauce, just thick enough to coat a spoon. Add mushrooms and peas and cook another 2 minutes.
Cook pasta, drain and shake out excess water. Thinly slice chicken. Add to pasta and gently toss with sauce, along with cheese. Serve immediately. Serves 8 to 10.

Pesto-Cream Sauce
¾ C half and half
½ T cornstarch
1 T butter
Grated Parmesan

1 C chicken stock
¼ C pesto
Salt and Pepper
Fresh Basil

In a blender, mix the half and half, stock, garlic powder, cornstarch and pesto. Melt the butter over medium heat. Stir in the half and half mixture. Simmer 2 minutes or so, until the sauce has thickened and warmed through. Season with salt and pepper and garnish with parmesan cheese and fresh basil. Serve over cooked pasta.

Pesto
2 C fresh Basil
2 Garlic cloves
½ C parmesan cheese

¼ C pine nuts
½ C Olive Oil

Combine in a food processor until thoroughly combined.

This recipe is from our sister Kerri who went through a creative cooking stage in her life that is best forgotten! (remember, she didn't graduate from gelatins for quite a while.) She sent this message with her recipe: "This recipe goes in the book especially for my sisters! When I was first married my husband gave me a cookbook and I vowed to try everything in it. I have never lived down, nor will I ever live down, trying this recipe and actually eating it. They always tease that it is one of my favorites!" We still think it secretly is and if she ever made dinner for her family, this would be a staple!

<u>Sweet and Sour Tuna</u>
Really! We've never tried this, but if you like canned tuna…

2 C (6 ½-oz each) tuna, drained	3 T vinegar
3 T butter or margarine	3 t soy sauce
1 large green pepper, cut in strips	1 can (20-oz) pineapple chunks
1 ½ C celery, diagonally sliced	2 chicken bouillon cubes **or**
2 T cornstarch	2 t instant bouillon
½ t fresh grated ginger	6 C cooked rice (2 cups uncooked)

Drain tuna fish; if packed in oil, oil may be used in place of butter or margarine, Heat butter or tuna oil in skillet. Add green pepper and celery; cook over high heat about 2 minutes. Measure cornstarch and ginger into 2-cup measure. Add vinegar, soy sauce, and syrup drained from pineapple; add enough water to make 1 1/2 cups. Add liquid to skillet along with corn starch, until bouillon cube is dissolved and mixture is thick and hot. Serve over cooked rice. Makes 8 servings.

Cashew Chicken

3 C boned, raw, skinless, chicken breast (about 1 ¾ pounds) cut into pieces half the size of your thumb. Mix with:

1 clove garlic finely chopped	½ t finely shredded ginger root
1 T soy sauce	1 T dry sherry
1 T cornstarch	1 T oil

Let stand at least 20 minutes before cooking. You can do this step hours or a day ahead and let meat marinate in sauce and spices.

Meanwhile, dice the following to about the size of a cashew:

½ C yellow onion	½ C bamboo shoots
½ C celery	1 pound fresh mushrooms

¼ pound Chinese pea pods/snow peas, string and cut in half large.

Gravy:

1 T cornstarch	1 T soy sauce
1 t sugar	¾ C water
few drops of sesame oil	1 C cashews

On high heat in wok or large skillet, sauté onions and celery with a little oil about 1 minute stirring constantly. Remove from pan and add a little more oil. Sauté bamboo shoots and pea pods about 1 minute, remove. Add a little more oil and sauté mushrooms; remove from pan.

Sauté chicken over red hot heat with a little oil until lightly browned and done, stirring and scraping the bottom of pan to minimize sticking. Divide into 2 batches to sauté if necessary to prevent slow cooking and watering. Do not over cook. Add mixed gravy ingredients and stir lightly until thickened. Return vegetables and mix; garnish with cashews and server over steamed rice.

You can substitute almonds, peanuts or walnuts for cashews and use bell peppers, green peas, carrots, and/or water chestnuts to taste.

Sweet and Sour Pork

1 lb pork loin cut into 1" cubes	1 t finely shredded fresh ginger
1 clove garlic minced	1 T dry sherry
1 T soy sauce	

Marinate 2 – 3 hours or overnight. Drain meat on paper towel, then coat with batter of:

2 egg yolks	4 T cornstarch

Deep fry at 420 degrees until crisp and golden brown. Keep warm in oven.

Sauce:

6 T sugar	2 T soy sauce
1 T dry sherry	3 T white wine vinegar
½ C pineapple juice	3 T tomato paste
½ C water	2 T cornstarch
½ t fresh ginger	

Combine all ingredients in saucepan and bring to boil stirring constantly.

Vegetables:

½ C green pepper cut into strips	½ C sliced carrots
½ C water chestnuts	½ C sliced bamboo shoots
½ C fresh pineapple chunks	½ C onion in chunks
¼ t salt	¼ lb pea pods

Stir fry carrots, water chestnuts, bamboo shoots, and onion in a little oil until transparent. Remove from pan and add a little more oil. Stir fry green pepper, pea pods, and pineapple for only a minute until just warm. Combine vegetables and pork in sauce and serve over rice.

Chicken Teriyaki

6 – 8 chicken breasts or pieces	1 C soy sauce
1 C water	2 C brown sugar
3 cloves garlic	2 T ginger

Mix all ingredients and marinate several hours or overnight. Grill Chicken. Marinade can be used to cook rice in.

Egg Rolls

1 to 1 ½ C chicken, pork, beef, or shrimp finely chopped. Marinate in the following:

1 t finely shredded fresh ginger	1 clove minced garlic
1 t dry sherry	1 t soy sauce
½ T cornstarch	1 T oil
1 pkg egg roll wrappers	

Marinate finely chopped meat for at least ½ hour. Can be marinated overnight.

½ head cabbage	8 – 10 green onions
1 can water chestnuts	1 – 2 T dried black mushrooms
2 eggs	oil

Put mushrooms in water to rehydrate for about 20 minutes. Slice thin and put in bowl. Slice cabbage very thinly. Slice water chestnuts and onions thinly. Stir eggs in a bowl and fry in pan. Remove and slice thinly. Stir fry vegetables in hot skillet for about 1 minute, remove from pan. Add a few more drops of oil and cook meat until done. Mix in vegetables. Cool completely.

Place 2 – 3 T of meat mixture in center of each egg roll wrapper and roll up like a burrito sealing edges with a few drops of water on fingers. Fry in hot oil in deep fryer until golden brown.

Alfredo Sauce

1 cube butter	½ C flour
1 pint cream	1 C chicken stock
1 – 8 oz cream cheese	1 C shredded parmesan cheese
½ C shredded asiago cheese	cracked pepper

Melt butter and add flour; cook until smooth and bubbly. Add cream, stock and cream cheese cook until thickened. Add cheeses and pepper. Serve over cooked pasta with grilled chicken or ham and cooked peas or broccoli.

Pasta with Ham

1 C ham cut into strips	2 eggs
1 t onion powder	½ C olive oil
½ C parmesan cheese	1 box thin spaghetti
1 clove minced garlic	

Warm ham strips and garlic in skillet with a few drops of oil. Cook pasta until tender. Mix eggs, onion powder, olive oil, and cheese in large bowl. Add hot, drained pasta to egg mixture and mix to cook eggs. Add ham and garlic.

Crock Pot Chicken

6-8 boneless, skinless chicken breasts	12-16 pieces of bacon
Seasonings: salt, pepper, garlic salt	2 cans cream of chicken soup
1 c. sour cream	

Cut each chicken piece in half. Wrap a raw piece of bacon around each piece of chicken and put a toothpick in to hold in place. Season as desired using salt, pepper, garlic salt, etc. Place in baking dish and bake at 350 for 20 min. (Bacon and chicken will not be done!) Transfer chicken (leaving toothpicks in) to crock pot. Mix soup and sour cream together and pour over chicken. Cook on low for 4-6 hours. Serve over rice, noodles or mashed potatoes.

ॐ❦

When we were little girls, one of our favorite treats was when we got to pick out a frozen dinner from the grocery store. It didn't happen very often, and frozen dinners were different back then. We knew on frozen "TV dinner night," we would be able to eat our yummy dinners sitting in front of the television in the family room with our warm, foil, divided trays sitting on kitchen towels. It was a very special family dinner for us. One of our favorite frozen meals was pot pies. The whole house smelled wonderful when those were in the oven. If you are a fan of the frozen versions of chicken pot pie, you will think homemade is amazing. You get to decide how much chicken and what kind or even no chicken. Maybe you like the potatoes and carrots, but not the peas. No problem. You get to make it however you like. Make your own and you may never go back to frozen.

Chicken Pot Pie

⅓ C margarine
⅓ C flour
½ t salt
½ t pepper
2 C cut up chicken

1 pkg frozen peas
3 carrots sliced and cooked
celery seed pastry
¾ C chicken broth
⅔ C milk

Celery Seed Pastry:
2/3 C + 2 T shortening
4 – 5 T water
1 t salt

2 C flour
2 t celery seed

Melt butter add flour, salt, and pepper and cook on low until smooth and bubbly. Stir in broth and milk stirring constantly. Bring to boil; boil for 1 minute. Stir in chicken and vegetables.

Crust: Cut shortening into flour, seeds, and salt. Stir in water to make dough. Roll 2/3 of pastry into 13" square. Place in bottom and up sides of 9 X 9" pan. Place hot chicken mixture into pastry shell. Roll remaining dough into 11" square and top sealing edges. Bake 30-45 minutes at 350 degrees.

Sisterfamilyrecipes@gmail.com

Chicken Enchiladas
4 chicken breasts, cooked & cubed | 1 (8-oz) pkg cream cheese (light optional)
2 T. olive oil | 2 cups Monterey Jack cheese, shredded
½ C water | 1 (4-oz) can diced green chili, drained (optional)
1 clove garlic, minced | 8 (10 inch) flour tortillas
1 jalapeno pepper, chopped (optional)
1 C heavy cream (1/2 and ½ or milk optional)

Preheat oven to 375 degrees. Heat olive oil in large skillet over med. heat. Add the green chilies, jalapeno and garlic. Cook and stir until fragrant, add chicken breasts and cook until tender; remove from pan and cut into cubes. Place cream cheese and half of the Monterey Jack into pan with green chili and chicken drippings. As the cheese begins to melt, gradually stir in the water. Stir in chicken. Remove from heat. Spoon the chicken mixture into tortillas, and roll up. Place the rolls, seam side down, in a 9x13 baking dish. Sprinkle the remaining cheese over the top, and then pour cream over all. Bake for 30 minutes or until enchiladas are golden brown on top.

Chicken Burritos
6 Boneless, Skinless, chicken breasts | ½ C bar-b-q sauce
1 C salsa or taco sauce | ¼ C chicken stock
1 clove garlic | ½ t cumin

Place all ingredients in crock pot and cook until chicken shreds easily. Use to make burritos. Place a couple T filling on flour tortilla; add shredded cheese, sour cream, and more salsa. Roll up.

Fajitas
1 t ground cumin | 2 lbs meat (flank or skirt steak, chicken, or shrimp)
½ t black pepper | 2 pkgs Hidden Valley Ranch buttermilk recipe
½ C vegetable oil | ⅓ C fresh lime juice

Pierce meat all over with fork. Combine all ingredients and pour over meat. Cover and refrigerate overnight. Grill meat and slice diagonally. Serve with tortillas, salsa, sour cream, refried beans, and rice.

154

Chicken Wings

18 chicken wings	2 T vegetable oil
½ C soy sauce	2 T Catsup
1 C honey or brown sugar	1 Clove garlic

Wash chicken and drain. Sprinkle with salt and pepper. Mix other ingredients together and pour over wings on greased baking sheet. Bake at 375 for one hour.

Chicken Cordon Bleu

4 boneless, skinless breasts	1 C flour
paprika	garlic powder
pepper and salt	4 slices ham
4 slices Swiss cheese	oil
2 T butter	1 pint heavy cream

Mix flour and seasoning together in shallow dish. Heat small amount of oil and butter in skillet. Pound chicken breasts to ¼" thick; place cheese and ham on each breast and roll up. Dredge in seasoned flour and fry until golden in skillet. Pour cream over chicken, cover, and simmer for 20 minutes or until chicken is cooked through.

Chicken and Dressing

2 pks stuffing mix	1 can golden corn soup or 1 can cream corn
2 cans cream of chicken soup	6-8 chicken breasts or tenderloins (enough to cover stuffing)

Mix soup and stuffing mix in bottom of 9X13" pan. Place chicken pieces on top – boneless or bone-in. Top with glaze:

Whisk together and pour over chicken
3 T brown sugar	3 T butter melted
2 t spicy mustard	

Bake at 400 degrees for 45 minutes.

155

Hawaiian Ham and Cheese Sandwiches

1 T poppy seeds	1 lb shaved black forest ham
½ lb sliced Swiss cheese	2 cubes melted butter
2 T Worcestershire sauce	½ t garlic salt
2 dozen Kings Hawaiian Sweet dinner rolls	

Slice rolls (cut one whole dozen at one time, leave sides stuck together to save time). Place bottom half of rolls in a glass baking dish, (9X13 will hold 1 doz) and top with ham and cheese. Place top half of rolls over the ham and cheese. Mix Worcestershire sauce, garlic salt and poppy seeds into the melted butter. Pour the mixture over the top of the rolls. Cover well and refrigerate overnight. Bake at 350 degrees for 15-20 minutes, or until cheese is melted. (letting them soak overnight is what makes them yummy)

Chicken Crescent Rolls

8 oz cream cheese	1 – 4oz can mushrooms
2 C cooked, cubed chicken	salt and pepper
2 cans crescent rolls	¼ C chopped walnuts
1 C seasoned stuffing mix	1 Cube melted butter

Mix cream cheese, mushrooms, chicken and seasoning. Spoon ¼ C mixture onto each crescent roll. Roll up and seal edges. Dip into melted butter then into nut and stuffing mixture. Bake at 325 for 30 minutes.

Chicken Salad

3 C cooked, chopped chicken	⅓ C mayonnaise
1 t onion powder	1 – 11oz can mandarin oranges, drained
1 t salt	1 ½ C toasted almonds
1 C thinly sliced celery	1 C seedless grapes, sliced in half
2 T lemon juice	

Combine chicken, onion powder, salt, juice, and celery; refrigerate several hours or overnight. Toss chicken mixture lightly with grapes, mayonnaise, oranges, and nuts. Makes about 6 cups or enough to fill about 18 croissant rolls.

Orange Pineapple Chicken Salad

5 c. chicken, cooked & cubed

1 can pineapple, chunks or tidbits

1 c. sliced almonds

2 t. curry powder

1 ½ C chopped celery

2 cans mandarin oranges

1 ½ c. mayo

Mix together and chill. Serve on bread or over lettuce.

Shannon's Favorite Chicken Salad

3 chicken breasts

tarragon

1 clove garlic, minced

2 C smoked almonds, chopped

Apple juice or wine

1 onion

salt and pepper

bread

Boil 3 chicken breasts in Chardonnay wine or apple juice (not water) with a little tarragon. After chicken has cooled; shred, remove bones (if bone-in chicken was used) and place in mixing bowl, add 1 small grated onion, garlic, tarragon, salt & pepper to taste and chopped smoked almonds. Remove crusts from bread and cut into desired shape. Spread chicken mixture on bread. Spread the top and bottom of sandwich with mayonnaise and dip into finely chopped smoked almonds, place on hot grill and toast.

New Recipes

Vegetables and Side Dishes

❧❧

Okay, we're not gonna lie. Vegetables are not one of our favorite things, well except for Jana who loves every vegetable and fruit she has ever tasted. You have to know that if the recipe is in here, it is amazing. We are difficult people to please. Maybe for book II we will be able to expand this portion of our cookbook. We are always on the look out for new recipes – they are just usually desserts.

Garlic Red Potatoes

2 lbs red potatoes, quartered
1/4 C butter, melted
2 t minced garlic

1 t salt
1 lemon, juiced
1 T grated Parmesan cheese

Preheat oven to 350 degrees. Place potatoes in an 8x8 inch baking dish. In small bowl combine melted butter, garlic, salt and lemon juice; pour over potatoes and stir to coat. Sprinkle Parmesan cheese over potatoes. Bake, covered, for 30 minutes. Uncover and bake an additional 10 minutes, or until golden brown.

Gourmet Sweet Potato Classic

5 sweet potatoes	1/2 cup white sugar
1/4 t. salt	2 T heavy cream
1/4 cup butter	1/4 cup butter, softened
2 eggs	3 T. flour
1 t vanilla extract	3/4 C brown sugar
1/2 t cinnamon	1/2 C chopped pecans

Preheat oven to 350 degrees. Lightly grease a 9x13 baking dish. Bake sweet potatoes 35 minutes or until they begin to soften. Cool slightly, peel and mash. In a large bowl, mix the mashed sweet potatoes, salt, 1/4 cup butter, eggs, vanilla, cinnamon, sugar, and heavy cream. Transfer to the prepared baking dish. In a medium bowl, combine 1/4 cup butter, flour, brown sugar, and chopped pecans. Mix with a pastry blender or your fingers to the consistency of course meal. Sprinkle over the sweet potato mixture. Bake 30 minutes until topping is crisp and lightly brown.

Scalloped Potatoes

8 medium potatoes, peeled	1 med. onion, chopped
1 lb bacon	1 C sour cream
1 can cream of mushroom soup	salt and pepper
1 1/2 C shredded cheddar cheese	

Fry bacon until crisp and drain well on paper towels. Discard all but 1 T. bacon grease; sauté onions in bacon grease and drain well. Slice potatoes thinly. Butter a 13x9 casserole dish; layer potatoes, bacon, onion mixture and finish with more potatoes. Cover with foil; bake at 350 degrees for 1 to 1 1/2 hours; uncover for the last 20 minutes.

෯෬ඏ

OK, weird name, but fabulous dish! This potato dish got its name from when and where it is used. When church groups make a dinner for the family of a loved one who has passed on, they want food in large quantities that is easy to serve and heat up. These potatoes fit the bill. They are easy to make, taste delicious, and feed a crowd. Don't wait for a funeral to enjoy them!

Funeral Potatoes

6 large potatoes boiled and peeled   1 can cream of chicken soup
1 small container of sour cream   2 C shredded cheese

Let cooked potatoes cool completely; shred into large bowl. Mix together soup and sour cream until smooth. Add a little milk to thin out. Add ½ C of the cheese and pour over potatoes. Stir to mix. Pour into greased 9X13" pan. Top with remaining cheese. Bake at 350 degrees for about 30 minutes or until hot and bubbly.

Oven Roasted Vegetables

2 medium zucchini   2 medium yellow squash
1 yellow onion   1 bunch asparagus
1 lb mushrooms   1 head broccoli
2 red peppers   2 cloves garlic
Olive Oil   salt and pepper
Basil

Cut vegetables into large chunks. Place on cookie sheet and sprinkle with olive oil, seasoning, and crushed garlic. Stir to coat each piece of vegetable. Roast in very hot oven at 450 degrees until vegetables begin to brown. Serve warm or cold.

Crispy Sweet Potato Fries

2 lbs large sweet potatoes   ¼ t salt
1 T olive oil   ¼ t ground black pepper

Wash and cut potatoes into wedges. Place in zip bag with oil and seasoning and shake to coat potatoes with oil. Pour onto cookie sheet and bake at 450 for about 35 minutes.

Sweet Potato Casserole
Mix the following together and place in greased casserole dish.

3 C cooked mashed sweet potatoes	½ C sugar
2 beaten eggs	½ t salt
½ stick butter, melted	½ C milk
1 ½ t vanilla	

Mix together and put on top
½ C brown sugar	½ C flour
1 C chopped nuts (We use pecans)	½ stick butter, melted

Bake 35 minutes on 350 degrees.

Paprika Browned Potatoes
6 potatoes	½ t white pepper
½ C flour	vegetable oil
1 T paprika	1 t salt

Slice potatoes. Combine dry ingredients in paper bag or zip top bag; add potatoes and shake to coat. Place on oiled cookie sheet and sprinkle with oil. Bake at 400 for about 20 minutes.

Oven Fried Zucchini
3-4 zucchini	parmesan cheese
Canola cooking spray	

Thinly slice zucchini and put on baking sheet in single layer. Preheat oven to 350. Spray zucchini with canola spray and sprinkle with parmesan cheese. Bake until crisp.

Grandma's Turkey Dressing

1 onion chopped	13 oz box of Dressing Mix
3 celery stalks chopped thin	3 eggs
salt and pepper	½ T thyme
¼ t oregano	1 stick butter, melted
½ t sage	Turkey neck, liver, heart

Boil neck, liver and heart until tender with 1 stalk of celery, half an onion, and a carrot. Use 1 C of stock for dressing. Remove the liver and mash up fine with a fork. Cook onion and chopped celery in butter until translucent (I also add sliced mushrooms). Combine all other ingredients in large bowl. Add 1 C stock, cooked vegetables, and butter. Mix and stuff into bird.

Honey Almond Couscous

¼ C honey	½ C toasted almonds chopped or slivered
2 T olive oil	1 C couscous
1 C chicken broth	

Bring oil, honey, and chicken broth to boil in small saucepan. Remove from heat and stir in couscous, cover and let stand for 5 minutes. Stir in toasted almonds.

Couscous is a great, quick cooking side dish that can be sweet or savory. I add dried fruit, parsley, herbs, vegetables, and other seasonings to go with whatever dish I am serving it with.

ର~ର

Our sister Marti got this recipe from her friend Beth Porter – She makes it for us every time we have a big family gathering. It is a family favorite with Mexican food! We must warn you when making it, it is like the loaves and the fishes, and it multiplies all on its own! It is so good, but you never run out, even the leftovers grow.

Spanish Rice

1 - 8 oz. can tomato sauce
2 T heaping (chunky salsa)
1 t salt

2 t butter
2 ½ empty cans from tomato sauce filled with water
½ small can diced green chills

Put the above ingredients in a medium sauce pan and bring to a boil. Add 3 cups instant rice. Turn off heat and wait 10 minutes. Fluff with a fork and serve warm.

German Potato Salad

2 lbs of cooked sliced potatoes*
⅓ C bacon drippings
1 t instant onions
½ t paprika

6 slices cooked bacon
¼ C cider vinegar
½ t salt

*Dell uses frozen hash brown potatoes instead of cooking the 2 lbs of potatoes & slicing them. Place cooked, sliced potatoes in large bowl; add bacon. Mix vinegar, bacon drippings, salt, onion, and paprika in bowl and pour over potatoes. Sprinkle with more paprika. Serve warm.

New Recipes

Breakfast

❦

Breakfast is one of our favorite meals, as long as it is after 10am! We love lazy Saturday morning breakfasts, or enjoying a leisurely late breakfast on a day off. Breakfast is a great meal at dinnertime too, and most breakfast recipes are quick, cheap, and easy. Breakfast is also a great meal to share.

Wheat Pancakes

We got this recipe from Joyce Tilly (who has since passed.) It is a great whole-wheat recipe, and so easy!

1 C whole wheat (not ground)
1 C milk or buttermilk

Blend together (in a mill or Blender) until very smooth and you hear no more grinding (about 3-4 min.) Important to have smooth now because after adding other milk it tends not to mix as well.

Add:
½ C milk
2 eggs
4 t baking powder

½ C oil
½ t salt
½ t soda (if you used buttermilk instead of milk.)

Blend for just a few seconds. The mix may seem thin but it thickens after sitting a few minutes. Cook on a hot griddle.

Best Ever Granola

¾ C brown sugar	1 C nuts (slivered almonds)
1/3 C vegetable oil	1 C shredded coconut (toasted ribbons are nice)
1/3 C honey	1 C dried fruit (we like craisins)
5 C oatmeal	¾ t cinnamon

Preheat oven to 375 degrees. In a small saucepan combine sugar, oil, and honey stirring occasionally until sugar dissolves. Meanwhile mix all other ingredients together; pour sugar mixture over and stir with large spoon to distribute it throughout. Spread onto a cookie sheet lined with foil and bake for 10 minutes, at the halfway point stir it around a little bit so that it doesn't get too browned. Let cool and then store in an airtight container. It will stay good at least 3-4 weeks, if it were to last that long.

French Bread Breakfast Casserole

1 loaf French bread	1 -8 oz cream cheese
6 eggs	1 pint ½ & ½
1 t vanilla	½ t almond
½ C sugar	

Cut French bread into 1" cubes. Place ½ of bread in a 9x13 greased pan. Crumble cream cheese over bread. Add other ½ of French bread over cream cheese. Beat eggs, sugar, flavorings and half and half; pour over bread. Bake uncovered at 350 degrees for 45 minutes. Casserole can also be covered and placed in refrigerator overnight and baked the next morning.

Praline Topping: As if this isn't a great recipe already, I added a praline topping after watching a cooking show with a similar recipe. It puts this fabulous breakfast recipe over the top!

1 Cube softened butter	2 C brown sugar
1 C quick cooking oats	½ t cinnamon (optional)

Blend together in a bowl with a fork. After casserole is completely cooked, crumble topping over top and heat under broiler until bubbly.

Breakfast Casserole

1 ½ bags frozen, shredded hash browns
6 large eggs
salt and pepper
¼ C water

1 lb sausage browned or bacon cooked
2 C shredded cheddar cheese
1 can crescent rolls

Grease the sides and bottom of a 9X13" baking dish. Open crescent rolls and spread evenly on the bottom of baking dish.; bake at 400 for about 8 minutes. Remove from oven and set aside. Crack eggs into small mixing bowl and whisk in salt, pepper, and water. Place potatoes and meat into large mixing bowl, add egg mixture and stir to coat. Pour potato mixture over crescent rolls in pan. Top with shredded cheese and bake at 350 degrees for 30-45 minutes

Overnight French Toast

3 eggs
2 T Sugar
¼ t nutmeg

1 C cream
1 t vanilla extract
French bread cut into ¾" thick slices

In bowl lightly beat eggs; mix in everything else. Place bread in a single layer on a cookie sheet. Pour egg mixture over bread and turn bread to coat both sides. Cover with foil and refrigerate overnight. Bake uncovered for 20-22 minutes at 350 degrees.

Buttermilk Biscuits

3 C cake flour
¾ t baking soda
6 T shortening

2 ½ t baking powder
½ t salt
1 C buttermilk

Heat oven to 450 degrees. Cut shortening into dry ingredients; add milk and stir until ball forms. Roll and cut biscuits. Place on ungreased cookie sheet and bake for 12 – 15 minutes.

Sausage Gravy

1 lb sausage
½ t pepper

¼ C flour
2 ½ C milk

Brown sausage; stir in flour and pepper. Add milk and stir and cook until thick. Add more milk if it is too thick. Serve over buttermilk biscuits.

French Breakfast Puffs

1/3 C butter	¼ t nutmeg
½ C sugar	¼ t cinnamon
1 egg	dash cloves and allspice
1 ½ C flour	½ C milk
1 ½ t baking powder	½ t salt
1/3 C melted butter	Mix ½ C sugar & 1 tsp cinnamon

Preheat oven to 350 degrees. Mix first 3 ingredients well. Blend flour, baking powder, salt and nutmeg, ¼ tsp cinnamon, cloves, and allspice. Stir in alternately with milk. Put in greased or papered muffin tins. Bake 20 – 25 minutes. Immediately dip in melted butter and then in cinnamon and sugar mixture.

Pat's German Pancakes

6 eggs	1 C milk
1 C flour	¼ t salt
¼ C margarine	

Place margarine in 9 X 13 pan and place in oven while it heats to 425. Place all other ingredients in blender and blend until smooth. Remove heated pan with melted butter from oven and pour batter into hot pan. Bake for 25 minutes in oven. Serve with syrup.

❧◈❧

We have to pause and give our sister Kerri some credit for this recipe. She gave this recipe to our family and the buttermilk syrup recipe. Unlike the sweet and sour tuna, these recipes are some of the best things we have ever put in our mouths. We have always made our own syrup and buttermilk syrup has almost replaced our traditional maple. She has definitely moved up in the pecking order for this one!

Oven Apple Pancake

1 ½ large Granny Smith Apples	½ C flour
½ C milk	3 eggs
5 T butter	2 t cinnamon
½ C sugar	

Peel and core apples, slice thin. Melt 3 T butter in bottom of pan of ovenproof fry pan. Fry apple slices in butter until tender. Mix flour, milk, and eggs until smooth. Pour batter over apples and place in 400 degree oven. Bake for 10 minutes. Remove and sprinkle with cinnamon and sugar and dot with 2 T remaining butter. Return to oven until brown. Serve warm with buttermilk syrup.

Corn Bread and Sausage Breakfast Casserole

Fry 1 lb of sausage links; coat bottom of 8" square baking dish with 2 T drippings. Arrange sausage in pan and spoon 1 small can of crushed, drained pineapple over and around sausage in pan. Sprinkle 2 T brown sugar over pineapple. Mix package of corn bread according to package directions, and spread over the mixture. Bake at 400 degrees for 25 to 30 minutes. Let stand 5 minutes. Turn pan over on a plate. Cut into squares and serve with hot syrup.

੨ঌ৵ঌ

Our Aunt Jane and Uncle David are fun and creative cooks and even more entertaining hostesses. Having a meal with them is a treat whether you are at their home, or they are at yours! Valayne's girlfriends and she took a road trop from Texas to Arizona and made a stop in New Mexico at Jane and David's. They had the best dinner and Sausage Apple Pie for breakfast! It was delightful! At dinner they all found a plastic animal at their plate that they had to use as the theme for a story, either real or made up, to share with everyone at dinner. They all had a great time! Aunt Jane and David collect things and Aunt Jane has a collection of napkin rings that baffles the mind! Uncle David made a special way to store them for easy use and access. You know you will have a fun time and great food with Jane and David! Stop by if you are ever in New Mexico. We are sure they will invite you in and show you a great time.

Aunt Jane's Sausage Apple Pie

Fry 1 lb sausage links. Make one pie crust for 9" pie pan by pricking bottom and sides of crust with fork after placing in pie pan and baking for 8 minutes on 400 degrees. Reduce oven to 375 degrees.

Pour a can (1lb 4 oz) of apple pie filling into crust. Arrange cooked sausage links spoke-fashion on pie filling. Sprinkle with 1 cup of shredded extra sharp cheddar cheese. For topping, combine 1/2 cup brown sugar, ½ C baking mix, and ½ cube softened butter; sprinkle over pie. Bake 25 to 35 minutes or until crust is golden brown. Serve warm.

Our aunt Jane says this is her boy's favorite breakfast but could be used as Sunday evening meal.

New Recipes

~ Syrups ~

We always made our own syrup. It seemed like the normal thing to us. We can remember the first time we had syrup bought from a store. It had a slimy consistency and didn't taste very good. We wondered why everyone didn't just make their own. It is so quick and easy. If you have sugar, water and some flavoring, you have all you need to make your own breakfast syrup. The basic recipe is just a simple syrup recipe of two parts sugar to one part liquid. You can combine sugars and use just about any liquid to make the flavor you want. Here's the basic recipe we grew up with:

Syrup
2 C sugar   1 C water
1 t Maple flavoring

Boil over medium heat for two minutes and serve.
You can use ½ brown sugar or all brown sugar for a slightly different taste.

Blueberry syrup – add 1 C fresh or frozen blueberries
Strawberry syrup – ad 1 C fresh or frozen strawberries
Apple Cinnamon syrup – add ½ t cinnamon and substitute 1 C apple juice for the water

Sistersfamilyrecipes@gmail.com

Buttermilk Syrup
1 Cube butter   ¾ C. sugar
½ C. buttermilk or canned milk

Heat in medium saucepan until sugar is dissolved. Then add, ½ t. baking soda and 1 t. vanilla. Syrup will bubble up. Serve hot on waffles, pancakes, and breakfast casserole.

Vanilla Syrup
1 cube butter   1 can evaporated milk
2 C sugar   2 t Vanilla

Melt butter and add can milk and sugar. Cook until sugar dissolves and it almost comes to a boil. Turn off heat and add vanilla. Serve hot.

Praline Syrup
¾ C Brown sugar   ¼ C light corn syrup
¼ C water   ¼ C pecans (toasted)
1 T butter

Boil first 3 ingredients. Reduce heat and simmer for 3 minutes. Add nuts and butter; serve.

Salads & Soups

❧◦❧

You may recall us mentioning we are not big vegetable eaters, and yet here is a whole section of salads and soups. Salad does not always mean veggies in our family. There is a lot you can do with a salad, and these are a few of our favorites.

There is nothing like a great bowl of soup on a cold fall or winter evening. We love soups. We have made them for weddings, showers, and family dinners for years. We are always on the look out for another great soup recipe. You can never have enough. Valayne is glad she has lived in places that have a lot of cold nights so she can make soup a lot longer than her Arizona family! She says she may be colder longer, but has the advantage in that she can also eat soup longer – She wins!

Sue Smith's Tortellini Salad
Cook a bag of frozen Tortellini (tri colored if you can find it) let it cool.

1 bunch of green onion (sliced thin)	1 red onion (sliced thin and chopped)
1 stalk celery (sliced thin)	1 red, 1 green, & 1 yellow bell pepper
Parsley (chopped)	(chopped)
Green olives w/pimento (sliced)	Black olives (sliced)
3 Chicken breast (grilled and optional)	½ C pine nuts

1 bottle of Paul Newman's Italian dressing
6 firm Roma tomatoes (cut into 1/6; fold in just before serving)

In a large bowl put fresh cooked Tortellini and pour over ½ the bottle of dressing. Refrigerate while cutting and preparing the rest of the vegetables. When all vegetables are chopped; stir into pasta and add the rest of the dressing and mix. Don't add tomatoes until ready to serve. Refrigerate.

Sistersfamilyrecipes@gmail.com

Shrimp Pasta Salad
1 bag Rotini (cooked, drained, cooled)
½ t onion salt
1 t garlic powder
Salt & pepper to taste
½ C Salad dressing
½ C mayonnaise

1 bunch green onions (chopped)
1 cucumber (sliced and cubed)
4 roma tomatoes (cubed)
2-3 pieces celery (sliced thin)
1 pkg baby shrimp (rinsed)

Mix together; onion salt, garlic, salt & pepper, salad dressing and mayonnaise to make a dressing. In a large bowl toss rotinni, onions, cucumber, tomatoes, celery and shrimp. Pour over dressing and mix until coated.

24-Hour Salad
1 can pineapple, crushed or chunk
½ C pineapple juice
2 (8oz) cream cheese
½ pint whipping cream, whipped

Juice of 1 lemon
2 eggs, beaten
1 lb. large marshmallows, quartered

Boil lemon, pineapple juice, and beaten eggs a few minutes. Add to creamed cream cheese. Add pineapple and marshmallows. Gradually add whipped cream. Refrigerate overnight or longer.

Paradise Salad
Mix together:
2 c. sour cream

2 (8 oz) cream cheese

Add 2 C each of:
Crushed pineapple
Coconut
miniature marshmallows

Mandarin oranges
Pecans

Chill and serve

Frog Eyed Salad

½ C sugar

1 t salt

1 beaten egg

3 qts water

8 oz Acini de Pepe

11 oz can mandarin oranges; drained

9 oz frozen whipped topping, thawed

1 T flour

1 C pineapple juice

2 t lemon juice

½ T oil

10 oz can crushed pineapple, drained

20 oz can pineapple chunks, drained

½ pkg miniature marshmallows

Combine sugar, flour, and salt. Gradually stir in pineapple juice and egg. Cook over moderate heat, stirring until thickened. Add lemon juice. Cool mixture to room temperature. Bring water and oil to boil. Add Acini de Pepe. Cook at rolling boil until done. Drain pasta and rinse with cold water. Drain again and cool to room temperature. Combine egg mixture and pasta, mix lightly but thoroughly. Add crushed pineapple, oranges, whipped topping and marshmallows. Refrigerate over night in airtight container.

છે∾ર્જી

Our mom's sisters are both fun and creative cooks – maybe it runs in the family. Tom and Erik love fruit and for many years we didn't sit down to dinner without this next salad recipe. It is not a family dinner without a fruit salad, and it is often this one we enjoy. It is quick and easy. It is also easy to keep all the ingredients on hand so you can make this salad at a moment's notice.

Aunt Barbara's Fruit Salad

1 large can fruit cocktail

1 can pineapple

1 bunch seedless green grapes

1 large sour cream

1 can mandarin oranges

1 can tropical fruit cocktail

1 large envelope instant vanilla pudding

In a large mixing bowl combine sour cream and vanilla pudding powder. Whisk together until smooth adding enough liquid from fruit cocktail to make a smooth, thick, sauce the consistency of pudding. Drain all cans of fruit and add fruit to sour cream mixture. Remove grapes from stems and add to bowl. Chill and serve.

Bow Tie Chicken Pasta Salad

2 boxes bow tie pasta	5 C chicken breast
2 C grapes, halved	2 C crushed pineapple (1 lg. can)
2 C diced apples	1 C green onion

1 bottle coleslaw dressing or 1 C coleslaw dressing & 1 C mayo
Cashew pieces

Cook and drain pasta. Let cool. Drain Pineapple and add to pasta. Stir in all other ingredients and chill.

Italian Pasta Salad

2 (16 oz) boxes Rotini, tri-color pasta	Red, yellow, & orange bell pepper
Red onion	Sliced olives
Cherry or grape tomatoes, halved	1 bottle Italian dressing
1 pkg. dry Good Seasons mix	1 C mayo
Salt & Pepper to taste	Parmesan cheese

Cook and drain pasta. Cool slightly. Dice onions and peppers and add to pasta in large bowl. Add olives and tomatoes. In separate bowl mix Italian dressing, dressing mix, mayonnaise, and salt and pepper. Mix well and pour over pasta mixture. Combine and top with cheese. Chill.

Buttermilk Ranch Pasta Salad

1 cucumber peeled and diced	1 package Farfalla pasta – cooked, drained, and cooled
2 avocados, diced	1 package grape tomatoes - sliced in half or quartered
1-2 cans sliced olives	1 package buttermilk ranch dressing

Mix dressing according to package directions.

Combine pasta, olives, cucumbers, and tomatoes and place in the fridge. Mix with dressing just before serving. Add avocado pieces just before serving.

Spinach and Blackberry Salad

9 C fresh clean baby spinach	2 T apple cider vinegar
1/8 t Worcestershire sauce	1 pt fresh blackberries or sliced strawberries
½ C almonds toasted	¼ t paprika
¼ C oil	1 t sesame seeds
2 T sugar	1 t poppy seeds

Toss spinach and berries together. Set aside. Place almonds in frying pan and toast on medium heat. Whisk together oil, sugar, vinegar, Worcestershire, paprika, sesame seeds, and poppy seeds. Toss dressing with spinach, berries, and almonds.

Red Onion Mushroom Salad
1 medium red onion - sliced
1 container mushrooms - sliced

Dressing

1 ½ t poppy seeds	1 ½ C sugar
¾ t dry mustard	1 ½ t salt
1 ½ C oil	¾ C red wine vinegar

Marinate the mushrooms and onion for 6 hours in fridge in dressing.

2 bags Romaine lettuce chopped	1 lb grated Swiss cheese
1 lb bacon cooked and crumbled	1 bag of sliced almonds
1 container cottage cheese (drained and rinsed)	

After the mushrooms and onions have marinated in the dressing, toss with salad and enjoy.

Poppy Seed Bow Tie Pasta with Grilled Chicken

1 C olive oil	3 T sugar
½ C sugar	1 lb bow tie pasta, cooked and cooled
½ C red wine vinegar	1 bag baby spinach
1 ½ t onion, minced	1 red pepper, sliced
1 t dried tarragon	1 red onion chopped
1 t mustard	1 can black olives, drained
1 T poppy seeds	1 can mandarin oranges, drained
1 C walnuts or pecans	1 grilled, seasoned, chicken breast, cubed
1 T orange juice	

Combine oil, sugar, vinegar, minced onion, salt, tarragon, mustard, and poppy seeds in blender and blend for 2 minutes until smooth. In a small saucepan, heat orange juice, 2 T sugar and nuts stirring gently until sugar is dissolved. Pour into small bowl and sprinkle with 1 T sugar. Spread on cookie sheet and bake for 8 minutes at 375. Cool and cover. Let cool completely. Mix remaining ingredients in large bowl. Pour dressing over salad and toss to coat. Sprinkle nuts over top.

Uncle David's Famous Salad and Dressing
Dressing
½ C mayonnaise   ¼ C sugar
1 T white wine vinegar

Mix and serve.

Salad:
Cooked bacon, crumbled   Broccoli – chopped and blanched
1 C shredded mozzarella cheese   1 C chopped walnuts
½ red onion chopped   1 head chopped lettuce (romaine works great)

Toss salad ingredients and top with salad dressing

Butterfinger Apple Salad
This salad is surprisingly good!

6 granny smith apples, peeled and sliced   1 can drained pineapple tidbits
1 container of whipped topping

Stir together, then add 2 butterfingers crushed, stir and enjoy.

Broccoli Salad
1 C green grapes   4 C bite size broccoli florets (blanched)
1 C red grapes   ½ C sunflower seeds
⅔ C slivered almonds   ½ C raisins
½ C green onions   1 C sliced celery
8 strips cooked, crumbled, bacon

Mix in large salad bowl and top with dressing:

1 C mayonnaise   ⅓ C sugar
1 ½ t vinegar

Red Wine Vinegar Salad & Dressing
Dressing
½ c. mayo   ¼ c. sugar
1 tbsp. Red wine vinegar

Salad #1- Iceberg lettuce, Red leafy, green leafy, slivered carrots cucumber, red onion, broccoli, small celery (tiny), cooked bacon, chopped pecans, red cabbage, can add mixed cheese-grated

Salad #2- Broccoli, red onion, grapes (purple) cut in half, sunflower seeds, raisins & bacon.

Taco Salad
1 Can Ranch-Style beans, drained and rinsed   1 head lettuce
shredded Monterey jack cheese   diced onion (optional)
Catalina Dressing   Corn chips
Chopped tomato

Toss together.

Sweet Basil Dressing
1/4 C red wine vinegar   1 tablespoon spicy/flavored mustard
2 T sugar   ¾ C pure olive oil
Salt and freshly ground black pepper   12 basil leaves, cut into chiffonade
1 Clove garlic

Whisk together vinegar, mustard, and sugar in a medium bowl. Slowly whisk in the olive oil until emulsified. Season with salt and pepper, to taste, and then stir in the basil and pressed garlic clove.

Creamy Balsamic Dressing
½ cup sour cream   Juice of 1 lemon
½ C mayonnaise   1 t Worcestershire
3 tablespoons balsamic vinegar   2 T Olive Oil
(I added a bit more at the end)   2 cloves roasted garlic
juice of one lemon   1 t sugar
Salt and Pepper to taste

Blend everything until smooth. Chill for one hour. Makes 10 servings

Sistersfamilyrecipes@gmail.com

German Potato Salad

2 lbs boiled sliced potatoes	6 slices cooked bacon
1/3 C bacon drippings	¼ C cider vinegar
1 t instant onions	½ t salt
½ t paprika	

Place potatoes and bacon in a large mixing bowl. Stir remaining ingredients together and pour over potato mixture. Stir to coat.

≈∽≪

Valayne loves potato salad. We have tried all kinds and have come up with a mix that we really like. The first time Valayne served this new potato salad at a family gathering was memorable. Our family does not really hold back when it comes to comments. Our sister Kerri took a big bite and we could tell by her face that she was not enjoying the salad. She looked at Valayne and asked if she had overcooked the eggs! She said they were hard and rubbery. She didn't realize Valayne had been chewing a piece of Swiss cheese!

6 potatoes, boiled, cooled and peeled (We like to use Yukon gold or something other than russetts)

½ lb Swiss cheese, diced	½ lb sharp cheddar cheese, diced
¼ lb thinly sliced ham, diced	1 ½ C mayonnaise
1 T spicy mustard	1 dozen eggs, hard cooked

Remove yolks from cooked eggs and place in small bowl. Dice cooked whites of eggs and place in large mixing bowl. Add potatoes, cheeses, and ham to egg whites in large bowl. Mix. Add mustard and mayonnaise to egg yolks and stir until smooth. Stir into potato mixture. Add salt, pepper, and more mayonnaise if needed. My mom doesn't think it is potato salad unless it has diced dill pickles in it. You can add those if you want. I sometimes use bacon instead of ham – just to keep Kerri guessing!

Croutons

Croutons work best with hearty, somewhat stale bread. Cube the bread and spread in a single layer on a baking sheet. Sprinkle with olive oil, herbs, salt and pepper. Bake at 350 degrees for about 15-20 minutes, until toasted. Keep in an airtight bag.

Cheese Broccoli Soup

¾ C butter
½ C thinly sliced celery
6 C heated chicken stock
8 oz cream cheese
½ C parmesan cheese

½ t onion powder
1 C flour
6 C milk
4 C steamed broccoli
½ C asiago cheese

Melt butter in large soup pot and sauté celery until tender. Stir in flour and stir until smooth and bubbly. Add milk, heated chicken stock, and cream cheese cut into cubes. Stir constantly until thick and smooth. Add salt and pepper to taste. Add grated cheeses and steamed broccoli chopped into small pieces. Do not boil, just heat through and serve.

9 Bean Soup

2 C of 9 bean soup mixed
1 tsp garlic powder
¾ tsp. pepper

2 qts. Water
¾ tsp. salt
1- 16 oz can diced tomatoes

As much or little of ham as you would like – the more the better

Soak beans overnight in water. Drain beans; add water ham and spices. Bring to boil reduce heat and simmer for 1 ½ hours. Add tomatoes and more salt and pepper to taste. Simmer another ½ hour.

Lentil and Sausage Soup

2 C lentils
2 quarts chicken broth or water
1 16 oz. can Italian diced tomatoes (optional)

2 links sweet Italian Sausage (cut out of casing)
2 links hot Italian Sausage (cut out of casing)

Cook sausage in large pot. Add the rest of the ingredients and bring to a boil. Reduce heat and simmer for 1 ½ hours.

Chicken Chowder

1 qt. broth
3 chicken bouillon cubes
¾ C grated carrots
6 potatoes peeled and cubed
Salt and pepper

2 chicken breast cooked (roasted add great flavor)
   and cubed
1 cube butter
½ C flour
1 can evaporated milk

Simmer the broth, bouillon, carrots and potatoes until tender; set aside. Melt butter; add flour salt and pepper, stir until thick. Add to the broth mixture; stir to thicken, add the canned milk. Heat through and serve.

Carol's Corn Chowder

1 C butter	1 onion, diced
1 carrot, finely diced	1 celery stalk, diced
1 clove garlic, minced	½ C flour
3 C white corn kernels, fresh or frozen	3 C chicken stock
2 C half-and-half	Pinch freshly grated nutmeg
Salt & pepper to taste	

Melt 1 stick of the butter in a large saucepan over medium heat. Add the onion, carrot, celery, and garlic, and sauté for 2 min. Add the flour and stir to make a roux. Cook until the roux is lightly browned; set aside to cool to room temp.

Meanwhile, combine the corn and chicken stock in another saucepan, and bring to a boil. Simmer for 10 min. Pour the boiling stock with the corn (a little at a time) into the saucepan with the roux, whisking briskly so it doesn't lump. Return the pan to the heat and bring to a boil. The mixture should become very thick.

In a small saucepan, gently heat the half-and-half, stir it into the thick corn mixture. Add the nutmeg, salt and pepper, to taste. Just before serving, cut the remaining stick of butter into large chunks. Add it to enrich the soup, stirring until the butter melts.

Quick Taco Soup

½ C onion, diced	1 – 14 oz can corn
½ C bell pepper, diced	1 – 14 oz can hominy
1 T garlic, minced	1 – 16 oz can ranch-style beans
1 T vegetable oil	1 – 6 oz can tomato paste
1 lb chicken, boiled and shredded	2 – 14 oz cans chicken broth
1 pkg taco seasoning mix	1 – 8 oz cream cheese
1 – 8 oz jar salsa	

In a stockpot, sauté onion, pepper, and garlic in oil. Add chicken, taco seasoning, salsa, corn, hominy, beans, tomato paste, and chicken broth. Simmer for 20 minutes. Put cream cheese in a separate bowl. Ladle hot soup brother over cream cheese to melt it. Add melted cream cheese to stockpot. Simmer for 10 minutes more. Serve in bowls. Garnish with tortilla chips and grated cheddar cheese.

Autumn Soup

1 lb ground beef	1 C chopped onions
4 ½ C hot water	1 C carrots, chopped
1 C celery,	1 C potatoes, cubed
2 t salt	½ t pepper
1 T beef bouillon	1 bay leaf
28 oz can crushed tomatoes	

Brown ground beef and onions together. Drain. Add remaining ingredients, except crushed tomatoes. Bring to a boil, cover and simmer 20 min. or until vegetables are tender. Add tomatoes, simmer for 5 min. Correct seasonings according to taste.

Clam Chowder

2 – 6oz cans of minced clams	2 C diced potatoes
¾ C flour	1 qt half and half
1 C diced celery	1 ½ t salt
¾ C butter	½ t sugar
pepper	

Pour clam juice over vegetables and add enough water to cover. Simmer about 20 minutes or until tender; drain. Melt butter, add flour and stir until smooth and bubbly. Add milk vegetables, clams, and seasonings.

Fire Roasted Tomato Soup

3 t butter	1 large onion (chopped) to make about 1 cup of chopped onions
2 cloves garlic	
1 can vegetable broth	2 - 15oz cans of Muir Glen organic fire-roasted tomatoes
1 t sugar	
½ C heavy whipping cream	2 T chopped fresh basil, cilantro, or flat parsley
¼ t crushed red pepper	

Melt butter, cook onion and garlic 2-3 minutes until onion is tender. Stir in tomatoes, broth, 1 tbsp basil, sugar and red pepper. Heat to boiling. Reduce, cover, simmer 15 min. Remove from heat, uncover, and cool 5 minutes. In a blender, place 1/2 of the mixture. Cover and blend. Add remaining. Cover and blend. Heat over medium heat until hot. Remove from heat and stir in cream and remaining basil. Sprinkle, if desired, with a garnish of basil and feta cheese.

Pumpkin Soup

2 t olive oil	2 shallots chopped
½ c chopped onions	1 ½ t grated ginger

Sauté until all soft. Puree in blender and add:

2 cups pumpkin*	1 cup orange juice
2 c chicken broth	1 t salt
½ t pepper	1/16 ground cloves

Simmer 10 minutes. Add ½ C of half & half cream, 2 to 3 T brown sugar, and heat.
*Roasted winter squash makes a great substitution.

Shannon's Creamy Jalapeño-Artichoke Soup

3 T flour	1 lg. onion, chopped
5 T butter	2-4 carrots, peeled and finely diced
3 C chicken broth	1 green bell pepper
2 C whipping cream	3-4 jalapenos, seeded & finely diced
1 C milk	2 cans artichokes - packed in water, drained & chopped
1 ½ C grated Swiss cheese	salt and pepper to taste
1 ½ C cheddar cheese	

Melt 5 tablespoons of butter in heavy large saucepan over low heat. Add flour and stir 3 minutes. Mix in chicken broth, milk and cream. Increase heat and bring to boil stirring constantly. Reduce heat and simmer until thickened, stirring occasionally, about 10 minutes. Meanwhile, melt 2 tablespoons of butter in skillet over low heat. Add onion, carrots, and bell pepper; sauté until soft, stirring occasionally, about 6-8 minutes. Mix in jalapenos and artichokes. Set aside. Add both cheeses to cream mixture and stir until melted, season with salt and pepper, then add vegetables.
* Note: if doubling recipe – double all ingredients except jalapenos, unless you want it toasty hot!

Stew

1 package stew meat (brown with flour in oil)

6 medium potatoes, cut and peeled	4 carrots peeled and cut
1 medium onion chopped	1 package frozen corn
1 can beef consommé soup	1 Tbsp Worcestershire sauce
1 Tbsp sugar	salt and pepper to taste
1 lb fresh mushroom	1 T Kitchen Bouquet

Add all ingredients to crock-pot add water and simmer until done. Stew may be thickened before serving by stirring in 2 T flour or cornstarch mixed with ½ C cold milk.

New Recipes

Appetizers & Dips

꤮꤮

We collect these recipes from everywhere and everyone. It is always nice to have the ingredients for something quick to whip together when someone drops by. How can you possibly visit without food? We know people do it, but we don't know why! These recipes all travel fairly well too. Who would want to go somewhere without taking something to eat with them? Some evenings you just don't feel like a full meal, so these dips and munchies are just the thing for those times. We are sure many of these will become staples in your home like they have ours. We guess you can get together with people and not bring food or have food, but why?

Shrimp Dip

1 – 5 oz can shrimp (chopped)   ½ lb. Cheddar cheese grated
1 C mayonnaise   1 t Worcestershire sauce
1 t parsley flakes

Combine ingredients; refrigerate. Serve with crackers.

Clam Dip in Sourdough Bread

10" round Sourdough bread   2 – 8 oz pkgs. Cream cheese
2 cans minced clams   1 T. El Pato
1 tsp garlic powder   ½ c. clam juice (drained from clams)

Slice lid of bread and hollow carefully. Mix remaining ingredients and pour into hollow bread. Put on lid and wrap in double aluminum foil. Bake 2 hrs at 300 degrees. Use additional bread chunks to dip.

Houston's Spinach Dip
Recipe from Amie

7-8 oz can marinated artichokes   10 oz frozen chopped spinach drained
½ t garlic (minced)   ⅓ C Romano cheese grated
¼ C parmesan cheese grated   1 C grated mozzarella
⅓ C half & half   ½ C sour cream

In food processor blend artichoke, Romano cheese, garlic, and parmesan cheese, just till blended, not pasty. In a mixing bowl mix; spinach, half & half, sour cream, and mozzarella cheese. Stir well. Add mix from the food processor into mixing bowl and blend. Spray ovenproof bowl with non-stick spray and bake at 350 for 20-25 minutes.

Artichoke Spinach Dip
1 – 13 oz can artichoke hearts, drained and chopped
2 ¼ C coarsely grated Monterey Jack Cheese
1 – 10 oz pkg. frozen chopped spinach, thawed, drained, and chopped
3 T freshly grated pecorino Romano cheese
1 C mayonnaise
1 C. freshly grated Parmesan cheese
½ C grated Asiago cheese

Combine artichokes, spinach, mayonnaise, 1 ¾ C Monterey Jack, and other cheeses. Stir to combine well. Transfer mixture to a 1 quart greased baking dish. Top with remaining Monterey Jack cheese. Bake at 350 for about 15 minutes or until hot and bubbly. Serve with vegetables, crackers, bread, or chips. This dip is great served topped with sour cream and taco sauce. Use tortilla chips to dip.

Spinach Dip
½ large bag of fresh spinach   1 C mayonnaise
1 C cottage cheese   2 bunches green onions, sliced thin
Salt & pepper

Cook spinach, drain well and let cool. Gently squeeze out the excess moisture. Cut it up with scissors. Blend mayo, cottage cheese & green onions. Fold in spinach. Season with salt and pepper to taste.

Serve with bread of your choice, or crackers, or chips or vegetables.

Crunchy Spinach Dip

1 C mayo   2 C sour cream
1 box frozen spinach, drain well   1 can water chestnuts, chopped fine
1 pkg Knorr or Mrs. Grass vegetable soup

Mix all ingredients in a large bowl. Cut out the center of large bread round and fill with dip. Cut removed bread into cubes and use for dipping. Also great with veggies.

Chili Cheese Dip

One can of spicy Hormel Chili (no beans)
Several dashes of hot pepper sauce
1 – 8oz pkg cream cheese

Place in microwave-safe bowl or small saucepan and heat through. Use with tortilla chips.

Sausage Dip

3 lbs Sausage   1 large onion - finely chopped
1 large green pepper - finely chopped   1 large tomato diced
2 cans chopped green chilies   2 cans chopped Jalapeno peppers
3 lbs cream cheese   16 oz sour cream

Cook up sausage and drain. Add onion, pepper and tomato and simmer for 30 minutes (drain) In a large pot add all ingredients and cook low for 3 hours, stirring when cream cheese starts melting every so often.

Creamy Crab Cheesecake

1 C crushed Ritz crackers   3 T butter melted
2 – 8oz pkgs cream cheese   ¾ C sour cream divided
3 eggs   1 t lemon juice
¼ t garlic powder   1 T El Pato Mexican tomato sauce
1/8 t pepper   1 C crabmeat

In a small bowl, combine cracker crumbs and butter. Press into the bottom of a greased 9" springform pan. Bake at 350 degree for 10 minutes; cool on wire rack. Reduce oven heat to 325.

In another mixing bowl, beat cream cheese and ¼ C sour cream until smooth. Add eggs; beat on low just until combined. Add spices, lemon juice, and hot sauce; beat until blended. Fold in crab. Pour over crust. Bake for 35-40 minutes or until center is almost set.

Cool on wire rack for 10 minutes and remove from pan to serving dish. Cool completely. Spread remaining sour cream over top and refrigerate overnight. Serve with crackers and bread selection.

Pesto Cheesecake
Crust:

1 C fine dry breadcrumbs	½ C finely chopped toasted pine nuts
3 T melted butter	

Filling:

2 C Ricotta Cheese	½ C half and half
2 T flour	salt
2 eggs	⅓ C pesto sauce

Preheat oven to 350. Lightly grease sides of 8 or 9" springform pan. Combine breadcrumbs, nuts, and butter in small bowl until well blended. Press evenly onto bottom of pan. Refrigerate until ready to use.

Combine cheese, milk, flour, and salt in medium bowl with electric mixer. Beat at medium speed until smooth. Add eggs, one at a time; beat until smooth. Pour into prepared crust. Spoon pesto, by teaspoonfuls, randomly over cheese mixture. Gently swirl with knife for marbled effect. Bake at 350 for 45 minutes or until center is just set; turn off oven. Cool in oven with door open for 30 minutes. Remove from oven and cool completely. Serve with crackers and bread.

࿇

Our friend Karen is the queen of dips and munchies. Her husband, John, does most of the "heavy" cooking in their home, but if you want some really great dip or something quick to eat you need to see Karen. We collected many of our dip and munchies recipes from her. John can grill anything and makes a pretty mean soup (see the soup section for some of his contributions), but Karen is the queen of quick and good food.

Chicken Wing Dip

2 – 8oz cream cheese	1 C blue cheese dressing
6 – 8 oz red hot sauce	2 C cooked, boned chicken shredded
1 C celery thinly sliced	8 oz Monterey Jack Cheese, shredded

Melt cream cheese in small saucepan; stir in dressing and hot sauce. Remove from heat; stir in chicken and celery. Pour into 13 X 9" pan and sprinkle with cheese. Bake at 350 for 25 minutes. Great with crackers, bread, celery, and anything else you want to dip into it.

Warm Cheese Dip
1 jar of extra sharp cheese spread 1 8oz cream cheese

Melt together in microwave and serve with bagel pieces. This is really yummy!

Texas Caviar
2 cans corn – rinsed and drained
1 can hominy
1-2 bunches chopped green onion
2 -4 tsp diced jalapeno (canned or fresh)
1 bunch cilantro
onion salt to taste
pepper
2 pkgs powdered Italian dressing (make 1

2 cans black beans – rinsed and drained
1 can black eyed peas – rinsed and drained
1 large can green chilies
12 roma tomatoes, diced
garlic salt to taste
crushed red pepper to taste
4-6 avocados, diced
pkg according to directions on packet)

Add corn, beans, black eyed peas, green onion, green chilies, jalapeno, tomatoes and cilantro, stir well, add seasonings to taste and 1 packet of Italian dressing. Stir well, then mix other packet of Italian dressing according to directions and add to mixture. Marinate overnight, add avocados before serving.

Salsa
2 large cans tomatoes
2 short yellow chilies
1 bunch green onions sliced
salt and pepper to taste
½ t cumin

2 long green chilies
2 jalapeño chilies
1 onion, chopped
2 cloves minced garlic
Fresh chopped cilantro

Mix all ingredients in a bowl and let flavors blend. Chill and store in covered jar.

Shannon's Salsa
2 16 oz. canned whole peeled tomatoes
Salt
2-4 cloves of garlic
1 can of diced green chillis
chopped cilantro

1 T vinegar
Sprinkle w/ salt & crushed red pepper
1-2 bunches green onion
1-2 t jalapeño, diced

Add 1 can of tomatoes, salt, vinegar, red pepper and garlic. Mix together, then add remaining ingredients in the order they appear. Mix how you like- a little for chunky and a lot for thinner.

❧❦

This is a great way to make vegetables go down easy! Mix them with some great cream cheese on a pastry crust and you hardly know you are eating vegetables! This is another great recipe from Karen. You can blanch cauliflower and broccoli to take some of the sharp taste out of those raw vegetables. They taste so much better. Just dunk them into boiling water for a minute then shock them in ice water and chop. They are great prepared that way for vegetable trays as well. This extra step makes a world of difference in taste.

Vegetable Pizza
2 cans crescent rolls
1 – 8oz pkg cream cheese
1 envelope ranch dressing mix
1 ½ C finely chopped broccoli
1 C chopped zucchini
½ C sour cream
1 C mayonnaise
1 ½ C finely chopped cauliflower
1 C chopped carrots
2 C finely shredded cheese

Spread crescent rolls out to cover the bottom of cookie sheet. Bake according to package directions until golden brown. Cool completely. Cream cheese, sour cream, mayonnaise, and dressing mix together until smooth. Spread over cooled crust. Top with finely chopped vegetables and cheese. Cut into squares.

Apple Dip
8 oz cream cheese
¼ C white sugar
1 C nuts, chopped fine
¾ C brown sugar
1 t vanilla

Mix together and serve with variety of apple slices.

Pumpkin Dip
½ can pumpkin pie filling
1 C powdered sugar
1 – 8 oz cream cheese, softened

Cream cheese and sugar together until smooth and creamy. Add pumpkin; mix until well blended. Use to dip ginger snap cookies, spice cake cubes, oatmeal cookies, etc.

Tang Fruit Dip
8 oz cream cheese
1 ½ c. cool whip
1 jar marshmallow cream
3 T. Tang

Mix together ingredients until smooth and creamy. Use to dip fresh fruit in.

Pina Colada Fruit Dip

8 oz. crushed pineapple, undrained
¾ C milk

Small pkg instant coconut pudding
½ C sour cream

Combine all ingredients in blender and mix well.

Lanie's Mango Salsa

Mango, red onion, tomato, cilantro, avocado, limejuice, salt and pepper. Mix in quantities to your taste.

Chili Cheese Ball

8 oz cream cheese
¼ t garlic powder
½ C finely chopped pecans

2 C shredded sharp cheese
1 – 2 dashes red pepper sauce
1 T lemon juice

Combine cheeses, lemon juice, garlic powder, and red pepper; beat with electric beaters until light ad fluffy. Stir in nuts. Shape into ball and roll in a mixture of 2 t chili powder and 2 t paprika. Chill several hours. Serve at room temperature with crackers.

Aunt Sylvia's Favorite Cheese Ball

(Makes two cheese balls)

12 ounces cream cheese
1 can diced green chilies
1 t onion salt

12 ounces mild cheddar cheese, grated
1 t garlic salt
1 t dry parsley flakes

Mix with electric mixer. Chill. Roll into balls and cover with chopped nuts. Wrap in plastic wrap and refrigerate until ready to use. Serve with crackers and breads.

Mom's Cheeseball

2 -8oz ounces cream cheese
2 T chopped pimento
1 T finely chopped onion
1 t lemon juice
Dash salt

2 C sharp cheddar cheese, grated
2 T chopped bell pepper
2 t worcestershire sauce
dash cayenne pepper
chopped pecans

Mix with electric mixer. Chill. Roll into ball and cover with chopped nuts. Wrap in plastic wrap and refrigerate until ready to use. Serve with crackers and breads.

☜☞

It is so quick and easy to make your own garlic bread/toast and it tastes so much better than anything you can buy ready-made in the store! Not to mention it is so much cheaper to make your own. We used to use left over hot dog buns, hamburger buns, whatever bread we had laying around or in the freezer. We prefer a hearty Italian loaf or French bread sliced on the diagonal, but any bread will do.

Garlic Toast

1 cube soft butter	1 clove garlic, crushed
fresh cracked pepper	½ t Worcestershire sauce
½ C parmesan cheese – grated	¼ C asiago cheese
1 t basil	½ t oregano

Blend all ingredients in a small bowl. Slice bread and spread butter mixture on each slice. You can either wrap the whole loaf in foil and warm in 350 oven, or broil tops in broiler until toasted.

Cheesy Bread

Round bread	Monterey Jack cheese
3-4 green onion, chopped	1 cube butter
poppy seeds	

Cut slits in bread both directions. Stuff cheese and green onion in slits. Drizzle butter and sprinkle poppy seeds over all. Wrap in foil and bake 400-450 for 10-20 min.

Cheese Biscuits

Dough:

1 ¼ C Baking mix	3 oz. freshly shredded cheddar cheese
11 oz. cold water	

Garlic Spread:

½ C melted butter	1 t garlic powder
¼ t salt	⅛ t onion powder
⅛ t dried parsley	

To cold water, add baking mix and cheese, blending in a mixing bowl. Mix dough until firm.

Using a small scoop, place the dough on a baking pan lined with baking paper. Bake in 365 degree oven for 10 to 12 minutes or until golden brown. While biscuits bake, combine spread ingredients. Brush baked biscuits with the garlic topping.

Crab Puffs

1 lb crab meat
½ t garlic powder
2 T. mayo
English Muffins

1 cube butter
1 jar Old English Cheese Spread
½ t seasoning salt

Combine all ingredients in bowl, mixing well. Spread on open English Muffins and broil until browned.

Herbed Oil for Bread

Fresh is best but use dry if you don't have them growing in your garden, like you should.
Mix equal parts (about 1 T.) of:
Basil leaves
Oregano
Parsley
Rosemary
Crushed red pepper
Ground Black Pepper
Kosher salt
Garlic

Stir together and put in an airtight container and keep in the refrigerator. Put 1 T of the mix on a plate and pour olive oil over mix and stir. Dip focaccia bread or Italian bread.

Flavored Oils

Place 1 C fresh herbs and 1 ½ C oil in small saucepan until oil is warm but not hot. Turn heat off and let oil cool. When completely cool, strain oil and place in clean jar.

Herb combinations:
Thyme and Rosemary (Mediterranean)
Garlic, Red Chili Flakes, Rosemary (Barbeque Marinade or Baste)
Cilantro (Mexican)
Peppermint, Garlic, Cumin, Coriander, Cloves, Fennel (Middle Eastern)
Red Chili, 2 cloves garlic, 2 bay leaves, 4 peppercorns, sun-dried tomatoes in olive oil

New Recipes

Beverages

✂◦✂

Sometimes you just need something great to drink. We don't drink alcohol, but sometimes you need more than a diet Pepsi at a gathering – although I would still rather have a large diet Pepsi with ice! We found these recipes to be fun and enjoyable. One we especially enjoy is our hot chocolate mix. We often started our day with hot chocolate and toast on a chilly Arizona morning. That hot chocolate was made with milk and cocoa by my mom on the gas stove, but we think our mix is just as good, maybe even better when you add a flavored cream.

Pina Colada Punch

Great for bridal and baby showers (for girls) and for Hawaiian parties.

1 quart Mr. T's (or any other brand) Pina Colada drink mix (without alcohol)
2 – 2 liter bottles of Cherry 7 Up.

Mix well and pour over ice. Serve

Hot Chocolate Mix

Another great gift idea. This is a staple in the winter in our homes. We keep a huge jar of it on the counter all winter long.

8 qt. box of instant dry milk	6 Oz. non-dairy creamer
1 lb powdered sugar	16 Oz. chocolate milk mix

Mix all ingredients together and store in an airtight container. Mix 1/3 c mix for each 1 c. hot water. This mix is really great with flavored non-dairy creamer. My favorite is caramel. Makes 60 cups.

Sistersfamilyrecipes@gmail.com

Hot Cider Nog
2 C half and half	1 C milk
1 C apple cider	2 large eggs
½ C sugar	¼ t ground cinnamon
⅛ t ground nutmeg	⅛ t salt
Cinnamon sticks	½ C whipping cream whipped and sweetened

Whisk together milks, cider, eggs, sugar, and spices in heavy saucepan; cook over medium heat stirring occasionally until mixture thickens and coats the back of a spoon. (about 15 minutes). Top each with a dollop of sweetened, whipped cream. Makes 5 ½ cups

Russian Tea
Boil and cool:

2 C sugar   2 C water

Add:
2 C orange juice	¾ C lemon juice
2 t vanilla	1 t almond extract
8 C water	

Serve warm. I find a large coffee make works great for making and serving hot drinks to a crowd.

Frappe
1 – 46oz pineapple juice	1 – 12oz frozen orange juice
1 ¼ C lemon juice	1 envelope powdered drink mix
1 pkg frozen fruit	3 C sugar
water to fill one gallon container	

Mix and freeze. Serve with 7-up.

Orange Julius
1 6 oz can frozen orange juice	1 C milk
1 C water	½ C sugar
1 t vanilla	12 ice cubes

Blend together in a blender until the ice is crushed.

Banana Crush Punch

4 C sugar
1 12-oz can frozen lemonade
6 C water
3-4 two liter bottles lemon/lime soda

1 46-oz can pineapple juice
2 12-oz cans frozen orange juice
5 very ripe bananas

To freeze: dissolve sugar in water. Add pineapple juice. Thaw frozen juices and add without diluting. Peel and mash bananas and stir into juice. Ladle into wide topped freeze container, leaving 1" head space. Cover tightly.
Freeze

To serve: Thaw in refrigerator to mushy consistency, about 4 hours. Mix equal amount of crush with equal quantity lemon/lime soda. Makes approx. 60 - 6 oz. servings.

Brazilian Lemonade

8 C Limeade made from concentrate   8 t of sweetened condensed milk
limes

Slice limes into circle slices and put inside the pitcher for color and flavor
Chill and serve!

New Recipes

Sistersfamilyrecipes@gmail.com

Contents

CPSIA information can be obtained at www.ICGtesting.com
Printed in the USA
LVOW041919290312

275320LV00008B/34/P